JOHN L. FITZGERALD

7 STEPS TO WEALTH

8TH EDITION

THE **VITAL** DIFFERENCE BETWEEN PROPERTY & REAL ESTATE

WILEY

7 STEPS TO WEALTH

8TH EDITION

"John presents an honest, time-tested strategy to wealth accumulation that every Australian should know about."

— **Michael Baragwanath,** Financial Planner

"I followed 7 Steps since 1998. My wife and I acquired 6 properties, sold 3 to fund our family home and now we've purchased our 4th investment property."

— **Jason McCartney,** Former AFL Player

"I started 7 Steps in my 50s. 20 years on, I sold just 1 of my 10 properties and made a $280000 profit from a $47000 deposit! Thanks to 7 Steps my retirement is secured."

— **Margaret Seedsman,** Former Mayor

"7 Steps works. We weren't property people when we got started, but we learned how to build a portfolio for our retirement."

— **David and Dada Bailey,** Engineer, Retired

"When I first read 7 Steps I didn't believe I could acquire multiple properties. I now have 13 properties and regret I didn't start sooner."

— **Craig Chu,** Banker

"7 Steps gives us a choice when to retire as opposed to 65 or 67 years of age."

— **Margaret Wachnik,** Business Owner

"To me, attitude is everything in life. 7 Steps gave me the right tools and attitude to help secure our future."

— **Wayne Dyson,** Corporate Coach

"As a leadership coach, I help people bridge the gap from where they are to where they want to be. Thanks to 7 Steps, I've learnt how to do that for my own retirement."

—**Toni Courtney,** Leadership Coach

"An insightful book delving into some investment property principles which all property investors should be aware of. The book offers some powerful insights into John's personal story and is a fantastic read for everyone embarking on their own property wealth accumulation journey."

—**David Shaw,** Accountant

JOHN L. FITZGERALD

STEPS TO
WEALTH

8TH EDITION

THE **VITAL** DIFFERENCE BETWEEN
PROPERTY & REAL ESTATE

WILEY

First published in 2018 by John Wiley & Sons Australia, Ltd

42 McDougall St, Milton Qld 4064

Office also in Melbourne

Typeset in 11/14 Sabon LT Std

© John Wiley & Sons Australia, Ltd 2018

The moral rights of the author have been asserted

A catalogue record for this book is available from the National Library of Australia

Cover design: Wiley/JLF

Cover image: ©vladars/Getty Images

Author photo: Moonboy Entertainment

House icon: ©Azaze11o/Getty Images

10 9 8 7 6 5 4 3 2 1

Disclaimer

The material in this publication is of the nature of general comment only, and does not represent professional advice. It is not intended to provide specific guidance for particular circumstances and it should not be relied on as the basis for any decision to take action or not take action on any matter which it covers. Readers should obtain professional advice where appropriate, before making any such decision. To the maximum extent permitted by law, the author and publisher disclaim all responsibility and liability to any person, arising directly or indirectly from any person taking or not taking action based on the information in this publication.

To my beautiful, amazing family; Maggie, Prema, Alex and Kane; and Ron and Suwanti Farmer; and our family of teachers and social workers at Toogoolawa Schools.
We are all teachers. Some teachers explain. Some teachers complain. Some teachers inspire.

CONTENTS

ACKNOWLEDGEMENTS

I first want to thank three Australian property billionaires, who are friends and colleagues I've known for a very long time, for providing their endorsement and taking the time to pick apart this thesis. It's rare for any Australian billionaire to endorse anyone as they are often very private people, but Bob, Nev and Maha all recognised the dire problem we face with growing welfare and inertia concerning how baby boomers are retiring.

Also thanks to my beautiful daughter, Alexandra, for painstakingly assisting with updating research and recommendations in this eighth edition. In the same vein, thanks to Nathan 'BG' Bowtell (Baby Giraffe), and Darren Marinovich and Brittani Pickering for all your help with logistics and data. Also, a huge thank you to Claire Louise Wright, wherever you are in this amazing world: thanks for all the foundations in earlier editions of 7 *Steps to Wealth*, which remain as building blocks today.

Finally, to the many thousands—or now tens of thousands—of 7 Steps practitioners who have followed me for more than 20 years and stand as testimony of this book as the best way to safely build wealth, reduce tax and ensure they retire comfortably without relying on the government: congratulations to you.

Land is the foundation of all wealth.

Albert Einstein said there are two ways to live your life: one is as though nothing is a miracle. The other is as though everything is a miracle. I believe in miracles and I give thanks and eternal gratitude.

PREFACE

This is not just a book about how to build wealth by investing in real estate. It's a book about how *you* can build wealth by investing in real estate.

There's a big difference. The words 'property investment' probably conjure up visions of serious guys in serious suits talking about things like 'negative gearing', 'leverage' and 'equity positions'. And for most people, that's a major turnoff. Perhaps that's why property investment is one of the best-kept secrets of the financial world.

I'm going to let you in on a few well-kept secrets in this book—and I'm going to try and do it in easy-speak language so that anyone can pick it up and read it. I figure, if Stephen Hawking can write a popular book based on Einstein's theory of relativity, then somebody ought to be able to do the same for real estate investment! I'd like to give you something you can relate to and, more importantly, use without constantly tripping over a load of jargon and statistics.

The books on wealth creation that are full of jargon and statistics (and there are a few of them about) are often written by academics who may have gathered a wealth of theoretical knowledge, but haven't actually—personally—created any wealth. I'd have to say, I'm pretty much the opposite.

However, Einstein himself said, 'Everything should be made as simple as possible, but not any simpler'. Good rule. So you will find numbers, charts and technical terms in this book, but they are there to clarify key concepts—not to prove that I can use statistics and big words. We'll also cover a fair bit of information, but this isn't one of those 'everything you never particularly wanted to know about economics' books. I'm simply going to tell you about the most effective way I know to build wealth.

By the time you finish reading this book, you will have a pretty clear idea of how to maximise your assets, reduce your tax bill, ask the right questions and see through some of the so-called experts in the field. And, perhaps most importantly, you'll know that you can build wealth.

The principles set out in this book aren't new. I've been using them for myself, and for clients, for many years—and they work. They've given us financial freedom, security and a great lifestyle for ourselves and our families. And that's just one part of what building wealth is about. For me, it's also about the potential to make a difference in the world: an opportunity to be all I can be. I think of it as a journey to discover purpose. Welcome to the adventure.

FOREWORD

As I write this foreword in early 2018 Australia is experiencing its highest sustained population growth and lowest interest rates in history. If ever there was a time for you to invest in property it is now, so if you've picked up this book really looking to learn how to safely and profitably invest in property, good timing.

If you've already read one of the seven earlier editions of this book and picked it up again I would also encourage you to read this version. You will notice new case studies of actual property investors, updated census data and fine-tuning of location criteria due to accelerated migration, foreign students and growth in healthcare as baby boomers retire. All these factors directly affect how we invest in real estate.

The 2016 census polarised a few important numbers for those of us who study property trends: Australia's population growth is at a record number, averaging 367900 per annum over the past 10 years. We struggle to build 180000 houses a year; 25 per cent of all homes are occupied by one person; and the average household population is fairly stable at 2.6, with 72.9 per cent of Australians living in a detached house. It's a fallacy that we are all living in apartments in the city. But what is polarising is that the main four capitals are attracting 78 per cent of the population growth and 87 per cent of the job growth.

The next big revolution will be AV (automated vehicles), which will completely change how we live. I make a point of studying this each year with the Urban Land Institute and have been considering the ramifications within my location criteria.

We are halfway through a property cycle. Different markets cycle at different times. After the first edition of this book, I started a group called Custodian, which acts like a buyers co-operative. We bought 416 properties for our clients in Sydney between 2011 and 2015 with an average price of $484 432, being house and land within 30 to 50 kilometres of Sydney's CBD and—most importantly, as you will glean from this book—we paid an average of $598 per square metre, and today the land is worth an average of $1313 per square metre. Our clients have made well over $100 million in five years. In the same time, the median house price has risen 85 per cent and apartments 73 per cent.

What's the most important advice I could give you? Well it's age old and comes from Confucius himself: 'Happiness comes from acquiring knowledge and putting it into practice'.

This book will give you all the knowledge you need. It's up to you to put it into practice. If you do, you will enter the realm of less than 1 per cent of all Australians. That's right: while 8 per cent of all Australians invest in property, less than 1 per cent do it properly, as you will learn in this book.

John L. Fitzgerald
Melbourne, January 2018

INTRODUCTION: A FOOL AND HIS MONEY ARE EASILY PARTED

There are really only two reasons why you would lose money in real estate:

1. greed
2. not doing your homework.

Unfortunately, those two things catch out about 95 per cent of 'punters'.

Greedy investors are usually locked into 'get rich quick' thinking—and they shoot themselves in the foot in all sorts of ways: making false economies, pricing themselves out of the market and selling short of real growth (50 per cent of property investors sell in the first five years). As an investor, unfortunately, you also need to avoid being manipulated by the greed of others—and there's a fair bit of it about in the real estate industry. That's why doing your homework is so important.

The real estate industry is huge: the residential sector alone turns over nearly $301.3 billion per year. That's a lot of property. And it's often bought and sold less on sound research and decision making than on sentiment, impulse, gut feeling and, of course, 'expert opinion'. (Multibillion-dollar industries seem to attract 'expert opinions' in about equal quantities.)

I forever have people walk into my office saying they've bought *the* property that is going to make them a lot of money, or that they represent a vendor or particular property that I've just *got* to acquire if I want to make money. Over the years, I have learned not to get too excited: probably one in 100 of these people has any idea at all what they are talking about.

It's a bit like McDonald's restaurants: everyone thinks they can set up a duplicate fast food chain because McDonald's make it look like such a simple business. It isn't—and thousands have failed in the attempt.

I'm reminded of this every year, on my pilgrimage to the AFL Grand Final. Everybody has a strong opinion about the game before, during and after it's played! Our opinions don't always coincide, and frankly, aren't always based on sober fact or objective analysis. That's our right to free speech! Sitting among the spectators, you could well believe that the person next to you would make a *far* better umpire than the umpire—and certainly a better coach than the guys in the box. The fact is, however, that umpires and coaches have paid their dues in the little league, or with other football clubs, and then graduated through the majors: they are appointed on their track record, and judged on their track record, game by game, as their career goes on.

The real estate industry has all the opinions—and not too many of the track records to support them. There are literally thousands of people giving advice about what to buy or sell, and quite a lot of them simply haven't got a clue! Others, of course, have their own good reasons for giving bad advice. And if you take that advice, you are probably a fool—and guess what will happen to you and your money?

It sometimes seems like there's a 'veil of mystery' (or perhaps it's just confusion) over property investment. If you're going to make good decisions that will build you wealth, you need to look behind two veils:

> **There are literally thousands of people giving advice about what to buy or sell, and quite a lot of them simply haven't got a clue!**

1. Why are you buying a property?

2. Who is selling or advising you to buy it and why?

There are really only three reasons to buy a property:

1. for *own* use — that is, to live or work in

2. for *income* — that is, to supplement your income in the short-term, through charging rent and taking advantage of legitimate tax deductions

3. for *capital growth*. That's what builds wealth. Add the dynamic of *compound growth* where you start with one property and use its capital growth as a springboard for acquiring more properties and you have solid potential for *serious* wealth.

I travel all around Australia talking to people about building wealth in real estate. A lot of them have already acquired some sort of investment property, and when I ask, they are quick to say: yes, indeed, of course they're after capital growth. But a few more questions usually reveal that they never in fact considered the capital growth potential of the particular property that they acquired.

They 'knew' that property goes up in value, but didn't realise that could mean anything from 20 per cent to 2 per cent per annum: in other words, the difference between positive and *negative* growth in real terms (in excess of inflation). They based their choice of property not on capital growth potential but on all sorts of other factors: they liked the idea of rental income (perhaps guaranteed by the vendor) or tax deductions; they 'liked' the property; it was recommended by someone they trusted; it promised low maintenance costs; it looked like a 'bargain'; or the finance offered to them on the property made it amazingly hassle-free.

None of these things make for capital growth. If you're looking to build wealth, look past them!

> **Do you want to know what the single most important factor for capital growth is? Land.**

Do you want to know what the single most important factor for capital growth is? *Land*. Land appreciates in value; buildings don't. However much you fall in love with a building, however low-maintenance it is, however much rent you can charge and however many deductions you can claim, the building will depreciate in value over time.

This is why so many investors get their fingers burned when they purchase new units or townhouses. The land content of their investment may be only 10 per cent of the purchase price, 90 per cent of which is therefore a depreciating asset. This is the best-kept secret of the real estate industry because no developer is going to tell you about it when they can sell 20 units instead of a single house or duplex on the same block of land.

That's why you need to look behind the second veil: who are the people selling you the property and what are they getting out of it?

The real estate industry itself ought to do some housekeeping, but it comes down to the old Latin principle of *caveat emptor*: buyer beware! Ask yourself a few awkward questions about the competence and track record of anyone selling or recommending a property and about their vested interests: what are they getting out of it?

You wouldn't believe, for example, how much heartache and loss of capital could be avoided by asking two simple questions:

1. Ask the agent to disclose the commission and marketing fees that the vendor is paying. Commission used to be regulated, but is now open slather in most states. It's a useful reminder that, no matter how cooperative they appear, agents work for the vendor (and themselves)—not for you, the investing buyer. Their interests—and those of their clients—are served by securing the highest possible price for a property: yours, naturally, are not.

2. Ask to see a copy of the bank's valuation of the property for security purposes. It is not always the same as the purchase price.

   You can't afford to be too trusting of the people you deal with. And that includes banks! Banks often lend on an investment property, knowing that the purchase price is way over their valuation of the property: they draw on your equity to make up the difference in the security, crippling your potential to build wealth (not that they disclose this to you!). Some banks do have a policy of disclosing. This should be mandatory. It isn't. Some investors don't find out until a year or two later that they have an unexpected deficit in the calculation of their net worth. I can assure you, banks would do things rather differently if their right to recovery were limited to their valuation of the property!

   > **You can't afford to be too trusting of the people you deal with. And that includes banks!**

Asking probing questions may be uncomfortable, but it's not nearly as uncomfortable as finding out that the equity you've built in your home over the past five to 10 years has been wiped out because you didn't ask the right questions.

You need to listen carefully to the answers, too. Many of them may well come into the category of lies, damn lies and statistics! For example, one of the tricks of the property trade is for marketers to justify sale prices and their claims of growth by quoting newspaper clippings and comparable investment sales. Companies have been selling units for years by claiming that there has been a 20 to 50 per cent growth in the value of similar properties—based on what other investors had paid six, 12 or 18 months before. But this is not a true reflection of the market. Investors aren't the true consumers of property—and what's to say that those previous investors weren't also talked into paying an over-inflated price?

Previous investment sales are often a barometer not of local market conditions, but of the effectiveness of a slick sales operation. My own home ground, the Gold Coast, has probably got the 'best' operators in this style: they sell literally thousands of properties each year to would-be investors at 10 to 30 per cent more than the market value using comparable investment sales to justify their prices.

And this is another reason to steer clear of units for investment: 60 to 100 per cent of all units built are sold to investors, not owner-occupiers. Which makes them a lousy barometer of market prices.

We'll discuss all these issues in detail later in the book.

So who's the expert?

I'm asking you to look behind the veil of anyone who has an opinion about investment property. So what are my qualifications?

Academically, none. But in 1985, when I was 22 years old, I started building a property portfolio that would have allowed me to retire very comfortably by the time I was 30. That in itself wouldn't make my advice better than the next guy's, but over the intervening period I have bought, sold or developed more than 15 000 properties, and I still develop more than 500 properties per annum. I have been doing this for more than 35 years and have a land bank of more than 14 million square metres.

I have learned by experience how to create wealth consistently—and how to use it sensibly. And I have successfully helped others to do the same.

Most Australian property investors buy, at best, one or two properties. My strategy teaches how to build a portfolio safely and efficiently. I have bankers who have accumulated 13 properties, mining workers with six properties, doctors with 17 properties and even single mums with seven properties.

In any case, I'm not trying to turn you into yet another 'expert' on property investment and management. I'd like to get you focused on *capital growth* and *compound growth*, just as a coach focuses a team on winning the game. I'd like to show you some of the pitfalls—so you don't have to fall foul of them the way I, and many others, did when we were starting out. And in the process, I may tell you a few things that don't usually get said in real estate circles.

Most importantly, I hope you'll realise that there are really *no* 'experts' when it comes to property investment. It's a bit like the weather: you can tell what it was like yesterday, and you might take an informed stab at forecasting what it will be like tomorrow, based on current trends—but you know that conditions are changing from day to day and from place to place. The real 'expertise' is recognising that you're no expert—and staying on the ball.

I don't expect you to take my word for anything. I'd like to give you the confidence to go out and ask questions, demand

Sceptics make the best wealth-builders.

evidence and investigate further. You won't be able to eliminate all your doubts or even all the risks: like any journey worth making, building wealth involves a few steps into unknown territory. But you can always test the ground. Sceptics make the best wealth-builders.

So that's what this book is all about

In chapter 1, I start explaining in detail how you can build wealth. By the time you reach Jason McCartney's story at the end of the book, you'll have absorbed a lot of information (although I hope it won't seem too much like hard work at the time). You may even have changed your thinking.

It's a real confidence booster to be able to see that happening. So please, take a minute to complete the short quiz at the start of Part I. You may already know some of the answers—but you may not. No worries; it's just like building wealth: you have to start somewhere! At the end of the book, you'll have the opportunity to do the quiz again. (And, as with building wealth, you may be surprised how far you get!)

WHO IS JOHN L. FITZGERALD?

This is another 'Introduction'—this time to me, and how I learned about building wealth. The point is, I'm pretty much an average person: if anything, a bit below average academically, and a bit above average in sport. I once bought a table tennis table ('flat packed for easy home assembly'). After half an hour of wrestling with the instructions, I found a nearby 15 year old who put the whole thing together, as advertised, in about three minutes.

If I can build wealth, you can. Seriously! And if that's all you really need to know about me, feel free to skip the next few pages and go straight on to part I.

I was born in Melbourne in 1963 and spent my first eight years in the middle-class suburb of Moorabbin. My father was a menswear retailer and he went into business on his own at the age of 30. By the time he was 37 he had built up three menswear shops in Collingwood, Belgrave and Stawell. He was a devout Catholic from an Irish Catholic family with five children, all in Catholic schools. My mother ran the home full-time, having left a career as a ballroom dancing instructor to marry Dad.

The school holidays of September 1971 changed my life—all our lives—suddenly and forever. My oldest brother David (then aged 12) went, as we often did, to visit Uncle Morris's farm near Shepparton. We heard later that he and our cousin Peter were lighting a fire when David, who was practising his notorious balancing act on a log, lost his balance and fell into the fire. Uncle Morris got him to the hospital, where he was found to have third-degree burns from knee to ankle and given skin grafts. I remember visiting David at the Shepparton hospital, with its slick lino floors and cold concrete walls.

He was there for six weeks. One Tuesday morning Dad drove out to visit him...and never returned. On the way home, his car was sandwiched between two semi-trailers and driven off the road. He was killed instantly.

At eight years of age, I sensed that there was a purpose behind those rollercoaster days: I believed, even then, that everything happens for a reason. That was the start of what I now see as a journey to discover my *own* purpose in the world—a journey that has since become linked to the creation and use of wealth. (If there's a 'bigger' purpose to you reading this book, I hope it will become clear as you read on.)

My mother had to take over the businesses, as well as run the family. She did a tremendous job, showing amazing business acumen for someone with no direct experience. To help her cope, we three boys were sent away to boarding school. I skipped Grade 6 in order to go to the same school as my brothers in 1974.

It was pretty clear from the first that I'd make my mark on the sports field, not in the classroom. I made the first 18 football team in form 4 (year 10) despite being a year younger than my classmates, and I excelled in athletics and various other sports—all rather costly in terms of academic achievement. I left school in 1979, having just scraped enough of an aggregate to get my HSC. I was expected to go to university, or to repeat my HSC to improve my marks, but I had decided that the academic life wasn't for me. Boarding school makes you independent: I had hardly lived at home since I was 10 years old, and the sum total of my worldly possessions fit into a locker 1.8 metres high by 40 centimetres wide. It was time to 'get in among it' and see what life was all about.

A friend and I had planned to hitchhike to Queensland (I wasn't old enough to drive a car, being not quite 17).

In January 1980, the friend pulled out… and I packed a knapsack and headed off alone for the Gold Coast.

The Gold Coast was in the midst of a property boom, and I immediately knew I wanted to be a part of it. I applied for several real estate positions as a salesman and eventually, through contacts, got a start with Bert Cockerel, who had an office in Surfers Paradise. To call Bert a 'Jack of all trades' would be an understatement. I remember going round to visit a motel he owned on the highway in Surfers called the Golden Sun Motel (now the site of a 30-storey high-rise tower called Zenith). Bert also owned the picture theatre at Palm Beach. And he was an avid fisherman, who used to do the fishing report on the local radio station! A great guy.

> **The Gold Coast was in the midst of a property boom, and I immediately knew I wanted to be a part of it.**

I went round to see him about signing my application for a licence as a real estate salesman. I had to disclose to him that I wasn't yet 17, but Bert wasn't fazed by technicalities. And neither, it seemed, was whoever rubber stamped the application forms: despite being up-front about my date of birth, I was duly and officially licenced for real estate sales. (Does that make me the youngest ever? Perhaps it's better not to ask.)

Less than a year after I joined Bert, I was introduced to George Margolis, who had built a fortune in real estate during the 1960s—and lost it in the crash of 1974–75. Now, he was re-emerging from bankruptcy and he had a good plan. With his knowledge and contacts, and my energy, we would make a tremendous partnership. So at 17 and 9 months old, I became an associate partner of Cousins Real Estate. I still didn't know anything about real estate. Fortunately, I was a fast learner.

Fortunately, I was a fast learner.

These were the heady days of the early 1980s: looking back, 'incredible' is the word that comes to mind. At my age and with my experience (neither one particularly impressive), I could advertise for people willing to invest in a private property trust to develop units and secure literally dozens of investors who were prepared to punt $50 000 to $100 000 on my ability to acquire a site, build a building and make a profit. As I said: incredible.

Of course, it wasn't just 'my ability': I had the building advice of a structural engineer who was part of the management team—and, of course, George Margolis.

Booms and busts, and bad decisions

I remember all too well the high-rise buildings going up along Old Burleigh Road and the Surfers Paradise strip, where units would be settling in a building such as Aquarius. The developer would attend settlement only to see the property transferred two or three times on the spot!

Greed, as always, was the underlying factor: real estate agents were promising that if speculators bought, they could on-sell the unit immediately because of the sky-high demand. It was not uncommon to see units sold off the plan by a developer for $150000 to $180000, re-sell for $250000, then $400000, then $500000 at settlement! (I call this the Bigger Fool Theory: if you invest in real estate on this basis, you have to be sure there's a bigger fool than you coming along to give you a back door.)

On the heels of greed, as ever, came the crash. In 1982, you couldn't *give away* high-rise units for love or money! Literally tens of millions of dollars were wiped off the (over-inflated) prices paid by investors at the height of the feeding frenzy.

> I call this the Bigger Fool Theory: if you invest in real estate on this basis, you have to be sure there's a bigger fool than you coming along ...

Developers also had their problems, notably Dainford Limited, which had built most of the high-rise buildings on the Gold Coast and had just completed the Peninsula building, the tallest and one of the best located buildings in Surfers Paradise. A record number of people had acquired the units on the basis that they could onsell them, found they couldn't and defaulted at settlement.

The ups and downs of the early 1980s taught me a lesson very quickly: real estate is an ever-changing market and while buildings are its prime 'product', it's the *land* that is the true, limited commodity. People repeatedly made the mistake of paying a premium above already over-inflated prices for a *building* that in itself was commonplace and easily replaceable.

Things haven't changed much: speculators are still madly snapping up inner-city units in Melbourne and Sydney, despite one in five currently having to take a *loss* on re-sale! (What percentage of Australians do you think buy units to live in as owner-occupiers? Take a guess.)*

*Just 6.6 per cent!

Becoming a wealth-builder

I acquired my first house-and-land package in Shailer Park, Brisbane, in 1985 for the tidy sum of $49000. I borrowed approximately $47000 on it—which sounded like a lot of money in those days. But that meant I could start out by investing only $2000 of my own money. That's where I started.

As at the start of 2018 that property is worth more than $650000. In fact, today the land alone is worth $650000. Let me break it down: I paid $15 per square metre for the land, for 1087 m^2 of land. Today, blocks around there as small as 300 m^2 are selling for $758 per square metre.

I had cottoned on to the fact that it was land that appreciated in value, not buildings, and that this created some rather encouraging mathematical effects: namely, if the house goes up by 10 per cent, the land will go up by 20 per cent. Armed with this information, and with a couple of houses under my belt, in 1987 I approached one of Australia's largest developers, Dainford Limited, and asked them to finance me into land estates. Dainford generally took 'long positions' in the market (that is, they committed to projects that wouldn't provide income for the first three to five years), so my formula for acquiring land and immediately turning it into income was pretty attractive.

Our first project together was a 1200-lot estate at Loganholme, south of Brisbane, which we acquired as an 'englobo' parcel (that is, land that has not yet been subdivided and where infrastructure has not yet been developed) for approximately $2500 per lot. Lots in that area at that stage were selling for around $25000, and houses for around $60000. As house values crept up to more than $140000, the raw land value rocketed to $90000, forcing the englobo land up to approximately $40000 or $50000 per lot.

This sounds like a complete sweetheart deal, but for wealth-building purposes, I wouldn't recommend it: land on its own generates no regular income (unlike a rentable property) and despite the potential for super profits, roughly nine out of 10 land developers go broke in any 10-year period. I was one of the lucky ones.

In four years, Dainford and I developed and sold more than 1000 properties together. Yet, for all that activity I realised I would have been a lot wealthier a lot sooner if I had constructed homes on 10 per cent of the allotments that I developed and sold, and kept them as rental properties.

I have probably made most of the mistakes that can be made — although I like to think I avoided a few through seeing them coming. I gathered a pretty good idea of what makes a good investment, and how to make a good investment work better. I realised you don't have to be a property developer to build wealth in property. (In fact, rather the reverse: most of them go broke at one time or another, pushing for bigger and bigger projects.)

Since 1994, my company, the JLF Corporation, has worked on a system — based on the structure outlined in this book — to facilitate wealth-building programs for 'ordinary' Australians. (None of them ever turns out to be 'ordinary' though.) We now hold public seminars on wealth-building for anyone who is curious about the concept.

From the start, we set out to do things a bit differently from other developers and marketing operations we know. We build relationships with our clients, beginning with their first property purchase. We've worked with those clients over the years, monitoring their capital growth and guiding them step by step to establishing a property portfolio.

And since 1998, our clients' properties have increased in value to well over $1 billion.

It's been fascinating for me to see people come fresh to the idea of wealth-building, and to see where they get to.

Some of the people we work with are top sportspeople who need to reduce their tax liabilities and shift their thinking from 'income' to 'wealth' for a future beyond sport. Others are those 'ordinary' Australians who may never have thought beyond paying off their own home and earning a decent salary until they retire, but for whom the words 'financial freedom' (or is it 'millionaire'?) conjure up a whole new world.

I am really proud of the fact that some of our clients, who started with us many years ago, are now up to five to six properties. Many have eight to 10 and some even have more than 10. We have one investor with 19 properties and a family with more than 30. In fact, the group I started for investors looking to build a property portfolio, Custodian, can boast having produced more than 700 millionaires to date. I don't know of any other organisation with such positive results. Likewise, there are tens of thousands — possibly even hundreds of thousands — of Australians who have read *7 Steps to Wealth* over the past 20 years and who have applied the strategies I've set out here. I get letters from readers and people coming to me at seminars and airports to say thank you, which is always great.

Becoming a Custodian

And there's another dimension to wealth-building, for me. Wealth-building is having a conscious strategy to acquire growth assets that will provide an income in retirement. Whatever our clients' initial motivation to build wealth — and I guess we all start out 'self-centred' about this to some extent — I've watched person after person achieve more than wealth through the journey. Many have also found perspective and purpose—definitely more than just financial rewards.

I had my own major shift in thinking along the way. As you may have gathered, I knew from a pretty early age that I wanted to be wealthy: I set some ambitious goals for myself, and went after them aggressively. I got there and then found that my perspective had changed.

There are very few wealthy people in the world. *Very* few. And I believe that it's pretty much up to those who control and enjoy the world's wealth to help those who don't. Once I had pulled myself into the former category, I felt the weight of that responsibility. I say 'weight', but I've actually found that the opportunity to use my wealth responsibly—to make a contribution to society—is one of the most joyful and enriching experiences of my life.

In 1990, I met a husband and wife psychologist team—Ron and Swanti Farmer—and together we established The Toogoolawa Children's Home, now Toogoolawa Schools Limited. Ever since, some of my wealth has funded this outstanding school, creating unique educational opportunities for troubled youth. You can read about Toogoolawa in Step 7.

When we, at Custodian, help people build wealth, we are not shy of urging them to think of themselves as custodians as well as creators: to think of wealth as an enabler in making a difference in the world. The choice of my company name was therefore no coincidence. 'Custodian' is what we are called and we live the values that the name implies—and we hope you will as well.

Custodian openly expresses its corporate mission and philosophy quite simply (see figure F1), and we encourage each person who joins us to become a fellow Custodian:

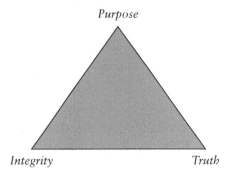

Figure F1: Purpose, truth, integrity' triangle

- *Purpose*: to create wealth
  to serve humanity

- *Integrity*: to accept responsibility

- *Truth*: to keep questioning.

Of course, none of this may be important to you right now. Feel free to put it all aside, but just let it idle in a corner of your mind somewhere for later. First, start building wealth so you and your family can meet your future needs—or to set yourself a challenge. And as you build wealth and meet your goals, perhaps you'll remember this seed of philanthropy sown here. Perhaps you too will find something more—something else to invest in for the future of our country.

On that note, let's move on to the business of building wealth!

PART I

STARTING POINTS

Quiz

Here are a few questions to help you focus on wealth-building, and to remind you where you are starting from. Don't worry if you don't know the answers yet: you will, by the time you attempt this quiz again at the end of the book!

1. In making a wealth-building investment decision, what would be more important?

    ☐ how you feel about it

    ☐ how it stacks up logically

2. What has shown the higher investment return over the past 10 years?

    ☐ shares

    ☐ residential property

3. In buying a residential investment property for wealth-building, what would be most important?

    ☐ rental returns

    ☐ taxation benefits

    ☐ capital growth

4. If you invested in residential property, would you use the same criteria and decision-making process as you used to acquire your own home?

    ☐ yes

    ☐ no

5. Is it prudent for you to acquire property close to where you live?

    ☐ yes

    ☐ no

6. What would be more important when acquiring an investment property for *wealth building*?

    ☐ managing your cash flow

    ☐ buying the right property

7. What type of property would show the highest capital growth?

    ☐ unit/townhouse

    ☐ house

    ☐ land

8. If you had a $300 000 deposit to invest in property, would you be better off buying:

    ☐ one property for $1 000 000?

    ☐ one property for $2 000 000?

    ☐ two properties for $500 000 each?

9. The median house price in Brisbane rose from $30 500 in 1977 to $550 000 in 2018.

    ☐ true

    ☐ false

10. If you bought a house in 1967 in Melbourne, Sydney or Brisbane, by how much would its value have increased in 2017?

    ☐ doubled in value

    ☐ five times (500%)

    ☐ 10 times (1000%)

    ☐ 20 times (2000%)

    ☐ 50 times (5000%)

11. Which institution(s) effectively control the affordability of housing in Australia?

- ☐ the Real Estate Institute
- ☐ banks
- ☐ property developers
- ☐ valuers

12. Is the number of renters of property in Australia increasing or decreasing?

- ☐ increasing
- ☐ decreasing

13. The Pay As You Go (PAYG) income tax (including Medicare Levy) on a salary of $60 000 is approximately $12 250.

- ☐ true
- ☐ false

14. Can I use my PAYG tax to build wealth?

- ☐ yes
- ☐ no

15. In choosing a location that is going to give capital growth, which factor is most important?

- ☐ proximity to transport
- ☐ proximity to schools
- ☐ percentage of investor-owners
- ☐ established capital benchmark

16. You are seeking a bank loan for an investment property. Rank the following criteria in order of priority.

☐ interest rate of loan

☐ interest-only loan

☐ full disclosure of bank valuation of investment property

☐ non-collateralisation of other property

17. What is the 'established capital benchmark' of an area?

☐ the median price of property in the area

☐ the highest price of property in the area

☐ the lowest price of property in the area

18. What was the average land size of urban houses in Australia's capital cities in 1970?

☐ 450 m^2

☐ 600 m^2

☐ 750 m^2

☐ 1000 m^2

19. What was the average land size of urban houses in Australia's capital cities in 2017?

☐ 450 m^2

☐ 600 m^2

☐ 750 m^2

☐ 1000 m^2

20. What was the percentage growth in the median price of a typical high-rise unit between 1999 and 2017?

- ☐ 4%
- ☐ 6%
- ☐ 8%
- ☐ 10%

21. What is the fastest growing employment sector in Australia?

- ☐ healthcare
- ☐ education
- ☐ manufacturing
- ☐ retail
- ☐ construction

Sorry, but I'm not going to give you the answers at this point! That's what the book is for. Forget about this quiz altogether for the time being.

At the end of the book, you'll get the chance to tackle the same questions again, with answers provided if, by that time, you need them ...

CHAPTER 1
Why build wealth?

Do you want to be wealthy?

Silly question, right? *Everybody* wants to be wealthy. Well, as a matter of fact, when we polled thousands of Australians 98 per cent said they absolutely didn't want to be wealthy but they did want to be comfortable. When we asked what that meant in dollar terms, most said they'd never thought about it. In fact, a July 2017 survey by Australian Unity and Imperica found that 77 per cent of all 45 to 64 year olds had not begun formal planning for their retirement.

Imagine what 'comfortable' should be: the security and the freedom. Imagine retiring with enough money to do all the things you've wanted to do, for as many years as you've got—and not having to rely on the government for a cent!

Let's look at it another way.

How much do you reckon you'd need—per annum—to live comfortably in retirement? I'm not asking you to do budgets and calculations and adjustments for inflation (although at some stage, if you're talking to an investment advisor, it would be a good idea). I'm just talking ballpark figures: what amount per year would you want to retire on, in today's dollars? Most of the people I talk to would say more than $70 000 per annum (even though the median wage in 2018 is closer to $80 000 per annum).

Your own estimate: $ _____ .

That estimate may be perfectly realistic for your own financial circumstances: you'd have to do a few calculations to find out.

You may be surprised to know that figure 1.1 shows what Australians actually *do* retire on.

Nearly all of us want to be wealthy—and nearly all of us retire below the poverty line! What's going on?

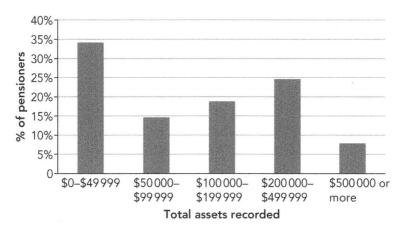

Figure 1.1: total savings and assets that Australians retire on

Source: Department of Social Services Demographics—June 2017 Release https://data.gov.au/dataset/dss-payment-demographic-data/resource/0457422b-f338-4dd8-82b7-35a5d97f798d

In order to retire on $70 000 per annum, you actually need around $1.5 million in assets *and* to own your own home.

And that's in today's dollars. In 20 years' time, with inflation at

> **Nearly all of us want to be wealthy—and nearly all of us retire below the poverty line! What's going on?**

3 per cent, the equivalent sum would be $150 000 per year, requiring $3 million in assets.

How many of us have a plan in place to build up those kinds of assets by the time we retire? Apparently, only one in 100 of us! As you can see from figure 1.1, more than 99 per cent will retire on less than one-third of what we need to be self-sufficient in retirement! If you are part of the other 1 per cent, please accept my congratulations—best wishes, and feel free to stop reading (although there may be a few things in this book that will surprise even you). If you are *not* one of those, it's *your* responsibility to change this for yourself! (Think about it. Who do you want to be financially dependent on when you retire? The government? Your kids? Read on ...)

Why aren't more Australians wealthy?

There are a number of answers to this question, as you'll see below. (I haven't included 'waiting to win the lottery'—although, with $75 billion 'invested' in gambling in Australia each year, you'd think we were pretty serious about this as a retirement plan!)

'We don't have enough money to build wealth'

Wrong. The structure I'll show you in this book allows you—even encourages you—to start small. You only need a combined annual gross income of $100 000 and a small amount of cash, or equity in your own home or other property, to get started. Wealth is accessible to most Australians. Mostly, it's about using the resources you have and restructuring your cash flow. And all that takes is (a) knowing how and (b) choosing to give it a go.

'Our parents never taught us to build wealth'

Most people my age were taught that we would grow up, get a trade or a university degree and then get a job: we'd save up enough money for a deposit on a house, and we'd use our work income to pay off the loan on that house over 25 years—and *then* maybe we could consider another investment. Sound familiar? Well, that's exactly what most Australians do.

I call this 'income thinking'. We need to replace it with 'capital thinking'.

'There's always a safety net'

I think this is part of the same concept. Our grandparents seemed to live fairly happily on the pension in the post-war years, and in the 1950s and 1960s, Australia enjoyed a relatively high standard of living compared to other nations. Of course, that was when there were about 18 taxpayers for every pensioner. Today, there are fewer than five taxpayers per pensioner, and if demographic trends continue, within 20 years there will be fewer than one taxpayer per pensioner. Meanwhile, because we're living longer, the average Australian will have to fund at least 20 years of retirement.

It won't be long before the government simply won't be able to afford the age pension—even at its current meagre levels. By 2020, welfare will cost Australia more than $190 billion per annum, up from $160 billion in 2017. That is staggering, and I'm sorry to say that unless you have a credible strategy, you are part of the problem. The government is fully aware of this—that's why in 2017 it stripped 320 000 Australians of some of their pension payments ($9000 per annum for singles and $15 000 per annum for couples). So we might like to think about making our own arrangements.

'We don't like debt'

This is something else our parents taught us. There are some sound values behind this view—self-reliance; pay your own way—and it's true that escalating debt is a concern. But we need to distinguish between debt on consumer items that depreciate in value (like a car, a dining suite or a stereo system) and borrowing on an asset that *appreciates in value* and *generates income* (like property). The latter kind of debt:

- supports the borrower's ability to make the necessary repayments
- offers a profit on sale of the asset.

On the other hand, you could buy a new BMW Cabriolet (say) for $100 000, and by the time you drive it out of the showroom, it's only worth $85 000. If you borrowed $100 000 on it, you're already facing a deficit of $15 000, which you have to pay off. Each year, more of the same: you could end up making payments of $12 000 for four years and still face a balloon payment of about $70 000 (which may, or may not, equal the capital value of the car by that time). Now, *that's* debt.

Ironically, people routinely run up thousands of dollars in 'small' debts on consumer items but baulk at taking on a mortgage.

Let's get debt into perspective. You can't build wealth without acquiring substantial assets for capital growth—and you can't, realistically, do that without borrowing the money to invest—that is, without *gearing*.

'It's an income world'

What does 'being wealthy' mean to you? Some people might say 'a big salary, with a lifestyle to match'. But that's not how wealth works. Income by itself doesn't make you wealthy. You spend some. You save some (maybe), and inflation gradually wears its value away. Capital, on the other hand, is material wealth that can be used to produce more wealth by investment. Capital grows, income flows (mostly, through your fingers).

Capital grows, income flows (mostly, through your fingers).

Unfortunately, most people don't get past income: they don't get their money growing and working for them. The system is there, but only capital-focused people use it to build wealth.

> **You can't save your way to wealth.**

You can't *save* your way to wealth.

'Wealth-building is strictly for whizz-kids'

Some investment advisors would like you to think so. But the good news is that property investment need not be the sole preserve of financial experts. By the end of this book, you'll know enough about 'leveraging' and 'negative gearing' to get by. You'll have a simple investment structure and clear principles to work with. And if the whole business seems like too much of a hassle, remember: you don't have to do it all yourself! You can get advice and help with everything from working out an initial budget to managing a whole portfolio of investment properties.

Custodian is just one example of an organisation that offers a whole range of services in the property investment field, or you could get advice from other sources. Look behind the veil. Try to find someone who has actually done what they are advising you to do! There's only truth in numbers: ask the person who is advising you to give you a copy of their land tax bill for the past 10 years. You want to follow somebody who pays a lot of land tax because clearly they own a lot of real estate. This goes for accountants, financial advisers and real estate agents. There are some good ones who have built wealth—and that's the first credential I'd look for.

'Wealth-building is strictly for sharks'

It's easy to get that impression—and not everybody relates to the idea that 'greed is good' the way we seemed to when Michael Douglas said it in the movie *Wall Street* in the early 1980s.

> **Sharing in the custodianship of our society's future is one way of being all you can be.**

I think we need to challenge the way we think about what wealth is for. Sure, it's about quality of lifestyle, providing for family, a financially secure retirement, control over your future and all that good stuff. But it is also about *responsibility*.

As I outlined in my personal story, the Custodian philosophy is that the few of us who are fortunate and informed enough to build wealth can—and must—choose to use it responsibly. Wealth puts us in a position to help those in trouble and need, and to shape the kind of fair and hopeful society we would want our children to inherit. It's also our responsibility to educate the next generation to manage and preserve capital for our nation's financial and social wellbeing.

Custodian believes that this is what true investment in the future means—and we find that it yields the most valuable and satisfying returns. We encourage all fellow wealth-builders to adopt this philosophy. This book is about what's possible in all sorts of ways. Sharing in the custodianship of our society's future is one way of being all you can be.

What's the solution?

At the risk of sounding like a sportswear advertisement, the solution is quite simple:

Just think differently: capital, not income

When we talk about 'wealth-building', we are talking about:

- establishing a *structure*, or system, to manage your *cash flow*
- acquiring *assets* (in this case, residential real estate)
- creating *capital growth*—that is, increasing the value of your investment over time.

Your investment may, of course, also offer you income and tax advantages. But it's the capital growth that counts. It's the capital growth—combined with compound growth—that makes millionaires.

And as it happens, most millionaires achieve capital growth by investing in real estate. This book will take you step by step through how it all works and what you have to do.

I'm essentially going to teach you how to turn $100 000, which could be the equity you've already built in your own home, into $2 million and be cash flow positive. On top of all that, you'll get a tax deduction. I hear you: it's too good to be true, or if it is true, why isn't everyone doing it? Yes, I hear that a lot. People who have been following me for 20 years say they wish they had started 10 years earlier and also ask why all Australians aren't doing it—and that's what stumps me as well.

> *Cash flow positive* is where you have income exceeding all costs of holding an asset.

CHAPTER 2
Why residential real estate?

If you look at any studies done over a 10- to 100-year period, you'd have to say that property seems to make good investment sense.

For example, it is, consistently, a major source of wealth for the wealthiest Australians (and 90 per cent of millionaires worldwide), as you can see in figure 2.1.

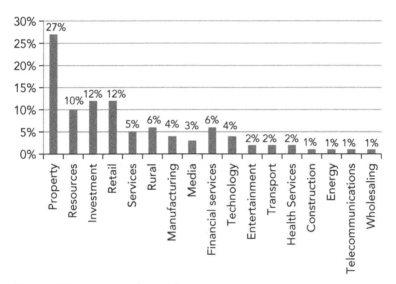

Figure 2.1: sources of wealth

Source: AFR 'Financial Review Rich List' 2017.

Residential real estate, in particular, scores pretty high on just about any quality you'd look for in an investment, remembering that your purpose is capital growth.

Let's have a look at all the boxes it ticks.

✓ Security

Residential real estate offers the security of 'bricks and mortar' compared to the fluctuating values of shares and commodities, and even compared to the manageability of commercial and industrial properties over the medium- to long-term. Even allowing for the ups and downs in real estate values we all hear about, the underlying trend shows remarkably steady growth.

You can see this trend quite clearly in table 2.1 (overleaf) and also in the graph in figure 2.2 depicting house prices in Sydney over the past 40 to 50 years.

In fact, the growth pattern has stayed pretty constant throughout the past century.

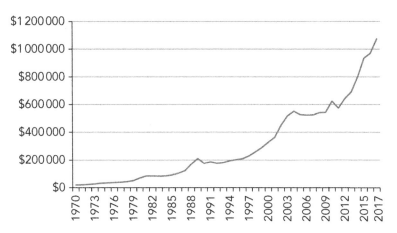

Figure 2.2: residential returns—Sydney metropolitan area

Source: Abelson & Chung (2004)—'Housing Prices in Australia: 1970 to 2003'; REIA (2015)—'REMF 1—Quarterly Median House Prices all Capital Cities from March 1980—June 2015'; Corelogic 'Home Value Index' December 2016 & December 2017.

Roughly speaking, this means that residential property has historically doubled in value every eight to 10 years. And don't forget that as the population continues to grow, the demand for housing must continue to increase.

Roughly speaking, this means that residential property has historically doubled in value every eight to 10 years.

	1976	1986	1996
Melbourne	$32900	$87000	$153000
Sydney	$36800	$104600	$210000
Brisbane	$26275	$59700	$135000
Adelaide	$29800	$73500	$110000
Perth	$33000	$56100	$127000
	2006	2016	2018
Melbourne	$375000	$720000	$832972
Sydney	$523000	$991000	$1048371
Brisbane	$326000	$537000	$532395
Adelaide	$286500	$448000	$458454
Perth	$395000	$512000	$483791

Table 2.1: house price growth

Source: Abelson & Chung (2004)—'Housing Prices in Australia: 1970 to 2003'; REIA (2015)—'REMF 1—Quarterly Median House Prices all Capital Cities from March 1980—June 2015'; Corelogic 'Home Value Index' December 2016, December 2017 & February 2018.

✓ Performance

The graph in figure 2.3 shows residential property as the best investment asset class over the past 90 years. And these are just averages. The better your real estate investment strategy is—where you buy, what you buy, how much land content you have and how you finance—the better the returns can be.

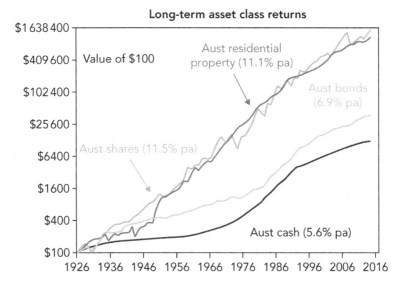

Figure 2.3: investment returns 1926–2016

Source: ABS, REIA, Global Financial Data, AMP Capital Investors

Some of the statistics actually downplay the performance of property. Take median house prices, for example. Over the past 20 to 25 years, the median house price in most capital cities has increased by between 8 and 11 per cent per annum. But look at that 'median house' in the 1980s: it's on a standard quarter-acre allotment, or 1000 m². Look at the 'median house' today: what with urban sprawl, the standard lot size has decreased to about 450 m²! Remember: it's the land value we're mostly interested in. If you look at the actual value of that quarter-acre block in the capital city, it has well outperformed the supposed 'median house price' and presented huge wealth-building opportunities, particularly with the advent of dual occupancy, or subdivision.

Remember the first house I bought in 1985? The land value has gone up 40 times, while the house-and-land value has increased 10 times.

✓ Leveraging

Because of its security and performance, residential real estate also represents 'security' (in the legal/financial sense) or collateral for loans. Most banks regard residential real estate as prime security against which some will lend up to 95 per cent of the property's value.

> *Gearing* is borrowing money for investment.

'Leverage' in mechanics is a way of turning a small amount of force, at a strategic point, into a much greater force. (Think of a car jack.) Financial leveraging works the same way: you can use a small amount of money to acquire an asset of much higher value on which you reap larger returns and growth. (This is a key factor in the performance of property, compared to shares, as a long-term investment. We'll look at it in more detail a bit later on.)

> *Leveraging* is gearing your investment so that the proportion of capital you invest is low in relation to borrowings: say, 20 : 80 or 10 : 90.
>
> *Equity* is your 'net worth': the value of assets that is actually yours, or accessible to you—in other words, the value of your assets minus the debt you owe on them.

If the value of an investment property goes up and the mortgage on it stays constant, your equity—or 'net worth'—increases.

Basically, the high degree of leverage on residential property allows you to build wealth by using just a little of your own money—and quite a lot of other people's!

This is great news because it means you don't have to be wealthy to build wealth! Residential real estate is actually one of the most *affordable* investments around.

You don't have to be wealthy to build wealth!

The banks' confidence in residential property allows you to use your increased equity as security in a fairly liberal way, to piggy-back one purchase on another and build up a portfolio of properties—as I'll show you in chapter 3—so that you benefit from compound growth.

What about shares?

A lot of people will try to tell you that shares are a better investment than property. It's true that some shares show a higher income return. They are easily tradable, and shares in the major companies have the advantage of high liquidity: they're practically cash. In fact, prior to the crash of 2007–08 shares even measured up to property based on annual returns. Obviously, that changed with the Global Financial Crisis (GFC) and the All Ordinaries Index falling by around 47 per cent. Shares are rebounding, but they have a long way to go—and property may equally well be at the peak of its cycle. So let's acknowledge that both show good capital growth. I'd still argue that property is the better investment. Why?

The difference is its *leveraging* ability. You can buy property with a 10 per cent deposit because it represents a bankable security. When it comes to shares, however, most banks will only lend 50 to 60 per cent of the purchase value.

Here's an example.

PROPERTY OR SHARES?

Bill and Ted each have $50000 in cash. Bill puts his down as a deposit on a property, while Ted uses his to buy shares.

Let's assume that in the first year the value of Bill's property increases by 10 per cent and Ted's shares go up by 12 per cent.

Which was the better investment?

Bill's property	Ted's shares
Deposit $50000	Deposit $50000
Bank will loan 90% = $450000	Bank will loan 50% = $50000
$500000 @ 10% capital growth	$100000 @ 12% capital growth
Return $50000	Return $12000

Bill's return is more than three times better in property.

Bill's *equity* has gone up from $50000 to $100000 ($550000 minus $450000). That's a return of just on 100 per cent.

Ted's *equity* has gone up from $50000 to $62000 ($100000 minus $50000), a 24-per-cent return.

Even if the shares have twice the 'growth' factor, the property offers more than twice the growth in true capital worth (equity) simply because of its leveraging ability.

Property's reliability makes a difference, too. When banks lend on shares, they usually reserve the right to a *margin call* should the shares drop in value. This can be scary because some banks can give you just two or three days to rectify the problem so if you have a falling share price, you could be topping up on a daily basis!

Even if the shares have twice the 'growth' factor, the property offers more than twice the growth in true capital worth (equity) simply because of its leveraging ability.

A *margin call* is where you are required to provide a cash top-up to maintain the agreed loan-to-security-value ratio. So if you borrowed 50 per cent of the value of shares and their price dropped, you would have to pay off part of the loan so that the outstanding amount still represents only 50 per cent of the value of the shares.

Banks *don't*, however, require a margin call on three-to-five-year property loans, particularly at the lower end price bracket. So there's no risk of them selling you up because of a temporary hiccup or glitch in the market!

What about commercial property?

Commercial property includes land and premises used for retail, offices, industry, entertainment and hospitality: anything from the corner store to the Westfield centre. While residential property values are expected to maintain their rising trend, the future for commercial and industrial property is much less certain, and that's generally reflected in the amount banks are willing to lend. Moreover, while the growing demand for rental property allows you to be a relatively passive investor in residential housing, you can't take the same kind of back seat with commercial property.

When you buy a commercial property, you're buying land plus buildings plus goodwill. If the property is tenanted, its purchase price will generally be based on the rate of capital return it offers, which may be a far cry from the building's replacement value. Let me give you an example. A friend of mine used to develop Big Rooster (now Red Rooster) outlets. He purchased the land for around $80 000 and built the premises for around $100 000, with car parking and landscaping and so on. He then leased it to Big Rooster for a whopping $40 000 to $45 000 per annum, and onsold it, showing a 10 per cent return. This is good development business.

The point is that an investor buying a Red Rooster outlet is paying a premium of $200 000 for goodwill, in effect, for Red Rooster's continued success. But if Red Rooster left those premises at the end of the lease, you would be left with an empty shell, with a replacement value half of what you paid for it, and limited ability to attract new tenants, since it was purpose-built for a particular fast food chain.

There have been some real horror stories since the GFC. For example, people borrowed to invest in companies that no longer exist, such as Westpoint, Timbercorp, Great Southern and Storm Financial. Tens of thousands of investors were burned.

Horror stories about margin calls are not just related to the companies that went broke. They also relate to the big 'blue chip' companies, whose shares also lost significant value. This made the banks call on their margins and investors had to come up with the cash within two to three days. In many circumstances, the banks sold the shares and then pursued those investors for the balance of their outstanding debt. This resulted in some people having to sell other assets or even their own homes. From my perspective, margin loans are a very high-risk way of investing in shares and making money, especially if you do not have the cash to meet the margin difference.

I remember an investor telling me he had found the perfect way to build wealth. He had bought large tracts of land and leased them for a 10-per-cent return to the emerging timber companies Timbercorp and Great Southern. He said he could buy these properties for $800 000 and with the timber companies renting them at 10 per cent, he could see no better way to make money. I told him the Red Rooster story — how they were bought out and closed many of their shops — and I suggested it was unwise to put all his eggs in one basket, especially in an industry as fickle as growing trees supported by tax savings.

Early in 2009, both Timbercorp and Great Southern went broke. They ceased making payments and left investors with large areas of land with small trees growing on them. The land has almost negative value because it does not provide income in its current state and the cost of clearing the land to provide income would cost hundreds of thousands of dollars. Future use of the land would also be subject to council approval and potential rezoning.

Businesses come and go — and not just geographically. Think about the retail areas around you. The past 20 to 30 years have seen the mushrooming of regional shopping centres, which have squeezed out many strip shops and neighbourhood shopping centres. They come complete with entertainment and refreshment facilities so you can stay all day and pick up a few more impulse buys. And now the elephant in the room — or I should say, on the globe — is Amazon. Nobody really knows the effect Amazon will have on retail in the next 10 years but everyone recognises they are huge and will somehow change the face of retail as we know it.

> **Businesses come and go — and not just geographically.**

I am not saying all shops are bad; what I am saying is that I suggest leaving it to the specialists and big companies. Some of the biggest and best in the world do it very well and even so, they too experienced tough times during the GFC. It is a similar story with office buildings. For example, office tenants will come and go (particularly new businesses, as many small businesses fail in the first four years—and the risk is even higher during a downturn). In addition, office buildings can be difficult to lease and as the owner you may have to pay tenants an incentive fee to enter into a lease or pay for the fit-out of their premises, or both. This can be very costly. The better buildings will rent well but these are $10 million investments—not what you would call a starting point for average Australians.

Banks look at commercial property differently from housing. I have a sizable commercial portfolio, but I also have dedicated managers working on it almost full time. When the banks reviewed my debt levels during the GFC, they were not at all concerned about my housing debt, but they did ask me to get all of my commercial properties revalued and then they demanded I lower my loan-to-value ratios (LVRs) to below 70 per cent of the new valuations.

I am not saying commercial property is a bad investment, but it is a specialised one for a small investor. If you are keen, you could invest in property trusts with a range of commercial properties, enabling you to spread the risk of tenant downturns. However, while commercial property offers a reasonable income base, it does not have the best potential for capital growth or for duplicating your success to build a portfolio.

Meanwhile, the future for housing...

Fortunately, we all have to live somewhere. And the wonders of modern technology still haven't provided any alternatives to living in some form of 'housing'. (Indeed 'houses' are still the norm outside medium- to high-density urban areas.) We also know we have long-term housing growth because Australia currently has the highest population growth on record. This growth is mainly a result of immigration, which is necessary because we have an ageing population. Approximately 700 Australians are reaching the age of 65 every day and retiring. We need to fill the resulting employment void so the government is focusing on a strong immigration plan. This will go for at least 20 years as the baby boomers retire. In fact, we are not only short of houses now, but we will need a lot more homes over the next 20 to 30 years to cope with the growth needed to replace our retiring baby boomers in the workforce.

Aren't we already investing in residential real estate?

One of the things I like about residential real estate is that it is a known quantity for a lot of people. They may not be entirely comfortable with the language of finance and banking, leveraging and gearing, but they have *some* experience of the sector, especially if they own their own home. This can be pretty reassuring if you're sticking your toe in the shark-infested waters of investment for the first time: at least you *know* that you know how to choose and buy a home.

But…sorry!…this actually makes for rotten investment decisions!

It's a bit like taking up snow skiing.

If you haven't snow skied, it's a great sport (and if it's accessible to you, I recommend that you give it a try). I learned some of the basic principles when I was a kid, but only took it up again about 10 years ago, having water-skied for many years. And now, on my annual visit to the snowfields in Victoria or New South Wales, I'm constantly reminded of two things:

1. Snow skiing and water skiing may look vaguely similar, but if you try to snow ski the same way you water ski you end up on your face (or worse). The apparent familiarity makes you feel pleasantly confident, but it can also blind you to the fact that the principles and techniques involved are quite different.

2. Logic and emotion can give you conflicting messages—and if you're doing something that 'feels' risky, it's the feelings that shout loudest! When you're on top of a mountain, thinking about heading down, logic and science and the ski instructor and all those good things are telling you that to stay in complete control, you need to lean down the mountain, with all your weight on your downhill leg. Meanwhile, your emotions are telling you to keep your bum as close to the snow as humanly possible! It's easy to say 'go with the logic', and I'm the first to admit that, for a novice, hurtling down a mountain at 30 to 40 kilometres per hour doesn't feel 'in control' at all (and, yes, the temptation to lean cautiously back into the slope is fairly powerful). But that's the reason you see me, and a fair few others, losing control on the slopes and ending up with our bums *on* the snow. We let emotion, not logic or science, make our decisions for us.

And that's exactly how too many people invest in real estate. They take the (largely emotional) experience they have in choosing their home, and try to apply it to choosing an investment property. Logic and science go out the window—and so does capital growth.

So what *are* the right criteria to use?

Choosing a home

When we choose somewhere to live, we naturally go with our emotions, gut instincts and lifestyle choices, and quite rightly—after all, this is going to be our home. We walk into a place (possibly with our partner), having looked at several properties—perhaps not even knowing what exactly we're looking for—and suddenly we're in love. It's the place of our dreams (or it looks like it could be, with a little work).

I had exactly the same experience buying the property where I used to live. My fiancée and I had been looking for months, and because of our lifestyle we particularly wanted acreage land near water. On a rainy Saturday afternoon, I drove up the driveway of perhaps the 20th property I'd looked at. I got out of the car and knew instantly: this was the one. I made an offer on the place before I was halfway through the front door—and without even consulting my fiancée. Talk about risky decision-making. Fortunately, she had exactly the same response to the place when we went back together the next morning—and of course, we did eventually get around to going through cupboards, flicking switches and checking carpets.

Later, I pulled down that house and built another one, and I am the first to admit I completely overcapitalised on the place as an investment. Even so, it was a great way to buy and make a home! If you're happy in your own place, be happy. You need to feel at home where you live: it makes a huge difference to your work and other areas of your life.

But it's not the way to invest in residential real estate for capital growth.

Choosing an investment property ... not!

I always seem to get people coming up to me bragging that they've started 'wealth-building', and all excited because they've just purchased an investment property to take advantage of negative gearing and so on and so on. They sound like they've won the lotto and they want to tell me all about it.

They spoke to their accountant and bank manager, got the tick, and went off in search of a property. Their first port of call was the local real estate agent, because after all, this couple had purchased their home through him, and they'd got chummy over the years. And would you *believe* it? The *perfect property* had just come on the market, *just around the corner* from their home! Old Mrs Reid's house was for sale: she was moving into a retirement village—she'd signed a contract to purchase a unit. It was such a big house, and she couldn't look after it any more. And what a bargain! ('She's asking $500000, but I'm sure if you made a cash offer you could get it for $475 000 ...')

Our couple can't believe their luck. They've driven past old Mrs Reid's house a thousand times, always admired it, and now they not only get the chance to buy it, they can get it for a full $25 000 discount on the asking price! Within 30 days, they've got themselves an investment property ...

Does that sound like a dumb reason? It does, if your purpose is to build wealth.

Why did they choose this particular property? 'It's ideal: *we can drive by it every day on our way home from work!*'

Does that sound like a dumb reason? It does, if your purpose is to build wealth. (In fact, our couple has broken just about every rule in this book.)

And do people really *do* that? It sure looks like it. Of the Australians who own residential investment properties:

- 29.5 per cent invest within their own postcode!
- 92 per cent buy second-hand properties
- 50 per cent buy apartments
- 34.4 per cent sell within five years.

Wrong, wrong, wrong.

Choosing a property for capital growth

Here's where the logic and science come in. There are three questions you need to ask yourself if you want to invest in residential real estate for capital growth:

1. What *structure* will best utilise my cash resources to allow me to build a property portfolio in the shortest period of time?

2. What *sort of property* will give me the highest capital growth?

3. What *location* will give me the highest capital growth?

Unfortunately, most Australians who invest in property don't ask themselves even *one* of those questions—let alone all three—which is why 97 per cent of them don't maximise their capital growth or their tax benefits. And why only 1 per cent of them build enough wealth to retire on an income (in today's terms) of more than $60 000 per annum.

Just one more statistic: 72 per cent of all property investors only buy one property. *One* property won't make you wealthy. You need to focus on building a *portfolio* of five or six properties over 10 years. The good news is, this catapults you to the very top—that magic 1 per cent—of successful investors for financial security and freedom.

So it's time to ask—and answer—the three big questions. We'll start with structure in chapter 3.

A structure for growth

In order to build wealth, you need to:

- establish a structure
- acquire assets for capital growth
- duplicate the process to develop a portfolio.

Why do you need a structure? Because there are different elements involved in making your investment work. You've got to consider land and buildings, equity and loans, tax and tax benefits, rental income and outlays, and time. The mix and balance of all these elements needs to be just right in order to *accelerate portfolio development* and *maximise capital growth*—and it needs to be do-able time and time again. If you can work out what the 'best fit' is, and set it out as a simple formula, you can achieve predictable results without having to juggle all the balls in the air all the time!

And you can *duplicate* the strategy without having to rethink it every time! Remember: one property won't make you wealthy. You need to use the equity growth in that one property to acquire a second, third, fourth...a portfolio of properties *all* providing (compound) growth. *That's* when it gets exciting!

Building wealth using property is a bit like building muscle using weights.

There are a lot of different elements to building muscle.

The weights are only the *vehicle* you use to build the muscle. (Some people seem to think just owning weights is good for you—but it's using them, and how you use them, that counts.)

Technique is important. You need to use a weight that is within your capacity, and to lift it correctly, in order to stretch a specific muscle. Then you can gradually build up to heavier weights.

Diet is all-important to 'fuel' the exercise. You need the basic energy of carbohydrates, a reduced fat intake and an increased intake of protein for specific muscle growth.

Finally, *rest* is essential. Muscle actually only grows when resting after being stretched.

A weekly or fortnightly exercise routine incorporating all these factors would provide an efficient, effective structure to follow.

Okay, so back to wealth-building!

An effective structure for building wealth will incorporate the same kinds of elements:

- a 'vehicle' for building wealth—in this case, residential real estate. The *land* is the vehicle for capital growth, and the *building* is for generating rental income.

- a 'technique' that will maximise the effectiveness of the vehicle for your purpose (capital growth). You need to select a suitable vehicle: the *right property*, in the *right location*. And you need to start, and stay, within your *financial capacity*—at the bottom end of general affordability, where most people can afford a first property. As you see growth, you can begin to build up a portfolio—more properties, not more expensive ones.

- 'fuel' for your investment. With a basic level of available equity and income, you can secure finance. With the right property and the right lender, you can borrow 90 per cent of the purchase price. You put in just 10 per cent of the capital and access 100 per cent of the capital growth. That's the beauty of leveraging.

In order to make this work without draining your personal resources you need *income* from the property to service the debt. If you optimise the rental income and maximise the tax benefits available, you can effectively offset *all* your outlays: not just the loan interest, but also maintenance, rates, fees and so on. As long as your costs are covered, you won't be putting any strain on your cash flow—and you shouldn't be able to get into too much trouble! In other words, you're setting things up so that there's a lot to gain and not a lot to lose.

> **You're setting things up so that there's a lot to gain and not a lot to lose.**

Meanwhile, you need to let your investment 'rest' in order for it to grow. Over time, the value of the property (in particular, the land component) increases, and since your debt stays the same your *equity* also increases. Once you have a 10 to 15 per cent increase in value, you can use the extra equity to 'fuel' the purchase of a second property—and so on, and so on—using exactly the same formula, and with no further claims on your income or other assets!

At the end of a 10-year period, you can have built up a portfolio of, say, six residential properties this way. If they've shown sufficient capital growth (and remember, house prices have doubled every eight to 10 years over a century) you need only sell one or two of them to reduce your borrowings on the whole portfolio—which leaves you with strong equity in the remaining properties, plus the ongoing rental income from them.

The overall structure can be illustrated as shown in figure 3.1.

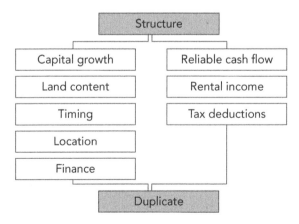

Figure 3.1: portfolio structure

If all this seems too good to be true, I'm here to tell you that it is possible and I'll be showing you how. Meanwhile, let's have a look at McDonald's as a perfect example of the structure in play.

MCDONALD'S RESTAURANTS

McDonald's is one of my favourite examples of a system based on real estate.

When Ray Kroc established the McDonald's franchise system in 1954–55, the menu consisted of only nine items, and the restaurants prided themselves in being able to sell and serve a 15-cent hamburger inside 60 seconds. By the end of the 1950s, there were more than 80 restaurants across the United States. Each franchise sold for around US$900 and franchisees also paid Ray Kroc a percentage of their investment as a franchise fee to cover administration. Unfortunately, huge business growth can't be sustained by limited capital—and therefore limited capital growth—and in the late 1950s, McDonald's nearly collapsed under its own weight.

So what enabled McDonald's to grow into one of the most outstanding businesses of the 20th century? Structured investment in real estate. The company acquired all the restaurant properties and then leased them to the franchisees, retaining management of some restaurants themselves. In the following decades, this strong real estate base financed the building of thousands of restaurants all over the world.

I am honoured to say that I've spent a bit of time over the years with Peter Richie, who founded McDonald's in Australia. I remember him telling me that one of the first stores they bought in Melbourne was on the Nepean Highway. It sits on 4000 m² and they paid $10 000 for the land back in 1970–71. Today that land would be worth $5000 a square metre. Do the math and you'll realise there's no better investment than land. In fact, I say it's the foundation of all wealth.

McDonald's is today worth billions of dollars because of a fundamental decision to restructure its cash flow, allowing it to acquire property and to secure a steady demand for tenancy (through the success of the franchise), thus generating rental income. McDonald's started out with little or no equity. That's pretty much how our structure works: supplying property to willing tenants (within an affordable price range) to finance the building of a real estate portfolio for sustained capital growth.

If you're interested, there is an interview I did with Peter Richie (first CEO of McDonald's Australia) on my YouTube channel: https://www.youtube.com/watch?v=gtYg15Fa5Ow.

How it all works: an overview

So let me try and give you a short summary of how wealth-building works:

- We buy assets that grow in value and provide us with income (cash flow).

- We borrow most of the money from the bank (gearing). The government actually gives us a tax deduction to do it.

- When the asset grows in value, we use the growth (equity growth) to repeat the formula—this is 'compound growth' and even Warren Buffet calls this the secret of all financial success.

Here's how it works.

Gearing

You borrow 90 per cent of the value of an investment property, giving you 10 per cent equity. All it takes is 10 per cent growth in the property's value and you have a 100 per cent return on the capital you invested, per annum! Figure 3.2 illustrates this.

Growth @ 10% $50 000

Loan $450 000

Deposit $50 000

Price $500 000

Figure 3.2: 100% return p/a on capital

Your 10 per cent could represent a cash deposit, or you could use the equity in your own home, which may be more tax effective. (I'll talk more about this in Step 4.)

Cash flow management

But what about the loan interest and all the other costs of buying property? Surely they eat away at your 100 per cent return? No: that's where the structure comes in. It's all about *cash flow management*: the basis of all successful businesses. See figure 3.3 (overleaf).

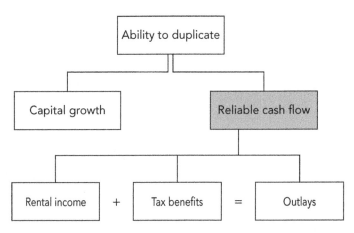

Figure 3.3: ability to duplicate

Equity growth

You need 10 to 15 per cent equity growth to give you the 10 per cent equity you need to duplicate your strategy for your next property. And repeat. And repeat again. The figures are illustrated in figure 3.4.

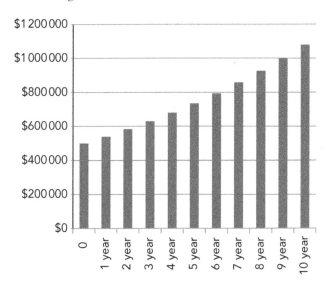

Figure 3.4: value and debt

If there's a warning bell ringing in the back of your mind about the *debt* you'll have chalked up by this time, don't worry: I promise to put that into perspective later on.

The starting point

You can begin to build wealth now if you have:

- about $100000 annual (combined gross) income *and*
- $100000 in available equity in your home or other property, or as a cash deposit (although there are ways of getting around this too).

And remember: you don't need to actually pay any of this out of your income. It's just an indicator of your ability to repay a loan: one of two criteria—as noted above—on which banks and other institutions lend money for property investment. In fact, you could actually increase your net income, thanks to tax savings, as we'll see in Step 3.

The beauty of compound growth

If I put aside just one cent and doubled it each day, how long would it take to turn it into a million dollars? The answer is: just 27 days. Sounds amazing, doesn't it? That's the power of compound growth: growth on growth (on growth ...)

Figure 3.5 (overleaf) shows how you can access that power from the starting points—$100000 income and $100000 equity—cited above.

Buy 6 homes over 10 years at 8% capital growth

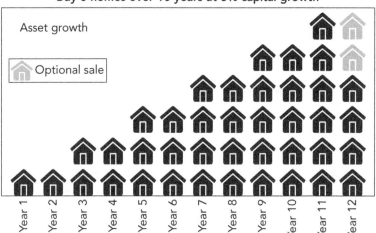

At year 12 net assets $2.81 million | Positive income $64 313 p.a.

Figure 3.5: financial goals—six properties over 10 years

How much can you achieve?

Figure 3.6 illustrates a slightly more aggressive use of the same structure.

I can't tell you what your goals or commitment should be or what your potential is. That's up to you.

My best advice is to allow yourself to start small and think big.

Over more than 20 years of coaching investors, I have seen many of my clients achieve six, eight, 10 houses…and more. Some clients have as many as 15 to 20 properties. They started small and built momentum. As the capital value of their properties and their income grew, they were able to duplicate to achieve compound growth. Many of them are now millionaires and multimillionaires by using exactly this system.

Buy 10 homes over 10 years, with option to sell in years 11 and 12

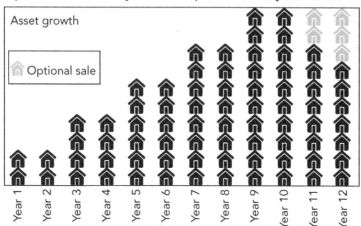

At year 12 net assets $5.33 million | Positive income $142 934 p.a.

Figure 3.6: financial goals—10 properties over 10 years

RIDING HIGH

Craig works for one of the top four banks. He first read *7 Steps to Wealth* in 2000 and came to one of my seminars. He didn't actually start investing until 2002 as, in his own words, he was overanalysing anything and everything. However, when his daughter was born, he realised he needed to take some action. He bought his first house-and-land package in 2002 in Aspley, Brisbane, for $285 000 when the market was running hot. By 2004 he had enough equity to enable him to purchase three more properties in Brisbane and Perth. As he became more comfortable managing his portfolio, he committed to investing further whenever he had borrowing capacity.

> Craig now has a portfolio of 13 properties in four states. More importantly, he has amassed 5900 m² of land in high growth urban areas and is cash flow positive. His portfolio has made him a multimillionaire and continues to grow by $300000 to $500000 per annum. The real opportunity will come when Craig retires in 10 to 15 years as he will be able to add more tenancies, such as granny flats, with councils now allowing much smaller lot sizes per dwelling in those high growth areas.
>
> Retirement income sorted!

You can watch Craig talk on my YouTube channel here: https://www.youtube.com/watch?v=hwYe_RMFzq0.

What does it take to make the structure work?

We've already mentioned the key elements, but let's now get specific. There are seven basic steps to building wealth:

1. buy land for capital growth
2. optimise your income
3. maximise your tax benefits
4. finance to build wealth
5. aim for affordability
6. make time work for you
7. be all you can be.

In Part II, I'll explain each step in turn.

PART II

THE 7 STEPS TO WEALTH

STEP 1

Buy land for capital growth

If you take away only one thing from this book, make this the one.

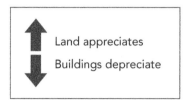

It's all to do with supply and demand. Land is a commodity that's limited in supply and for which demand is continually growing as the population increases. 'Bricks and mortar' is pegged to inflation and labour costs, so while its price goes up, it is not, as yet, in limited supply: buildings are pulled down (sometimes just before they fall down) and are easily replaced.

If you extract the land value from the growing value of house-and-land prices over a 30- to 40-year period, you will see that the land increases in value by nearly twice as much as the house. As a compound effect, in any 10-year period land shows capital growth of around 15 to 20 per cent, depending on location. The building component depreciates, effectively reducing the property's investment value—although inflation can camouflage the lack of capital growth. (During the 1970s, just about everything went up in value by 10 to 15 per cent per annum, but the lower inflation rates of the 1990s unmasked the real extent of land growth in comparison to the building cost, which is the house replacement value.)

As an example, figure S1.1 shows the growth in land-only value versus house-and-land value over the past 30 years for a property I purchased in Shailer Park, 25km outside of Brisbane CBD. I paid around $16 per square metre in 1985 and today lots as small as 300 square metres are selling for more than $750 per square metre. In fact, even if my land was vacant now, it would sell for around $650 per square metre as it is a 1087 m² block and can be subdivided or dual occupied (which means two houses can be built on the block). The house, which is now 30 years old, really isn't worth anything. While it's a 150 m² house that's given me good rental yield in a great location, it's really all about the land. (By the way, in that particular council I can subdivide or add a granny flat.)

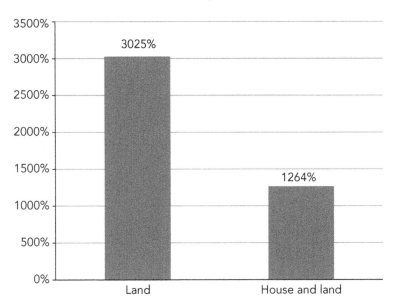

Figure S1.1: Growth in land-only value versus house-and-land value in Shailer Park 1986–2018

If you are starting out with limited capital, you can't just buy land: you need a vehicle for generating income to service your debt. That vehicle is *rental property*. But, knowing that the land is the appreciating component, you need to acquire rental properties *with the highest possible proportion of land content.*

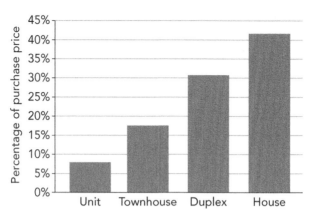

Figure S1.2: land content of residential property

Take a look at figure S1.2. In order to achieve real capital growth to enable you to build a portfolio over a five- to 10-year period, you need to have *at least 30 per cent land content.*

Duplexes and houses fall into the category of effective wealth-building assets, with 30 per cent (or more) land content. Townhouses within 7 kilometres of a CBD *can* also sneak into this bracket. (Check before you jump in.)

The 'good old' suburban home has the highest land content and invariably gives the best capital growth.

What about units?

I'll say it again: in order to achieve real capital growth over a five- to 10-year period, you need to have at least 30 per cent land content. For most units and townhouses, you'd be lucky if the land content is 10 to 15 per cent of the purchase price.

Say you bought a residential unit as an investment over a 10- to 20-year period, as some 50 per cent of investors do. The proportion of land value to building value is, perhaps, 10 : 90. Land appreciates, buildings depreciate,—so you end up with limited capital growth (other than inflation) for the first five to 10 years. This is *not* the way to start building a property portfolio.

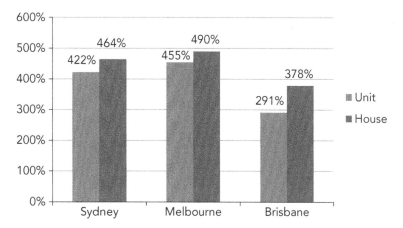

Figure S1.3: capital growth in the main capital cities, 1997–2017

Source: REIA (2015): 'REMF 1—Quarterly Median House Prices all Capital Cities from March 1980–June 2015'; REIA (2015): 'REMF 1—Quarterly Median Other Dwellings Prices all Capital Cities from March 1980–June 2015'; Corelogic 'Home Value Index', Dec 2017.

I have to tell you that the statistics don't support me on this one! As figure S1.3 shows, the median house price growth in Sydney, Melbourne and Brisbane has averaged 22.2 per cent simple growth and 7.72 per cent compound growth over the past 20 years. And units have averaged 19.47 per cent simple growth and 6.94 per cent compound growth. Compound growth is the key and with property it improves over time. I'm going to be talking about the power of compound growth in Step 6, but for now let me get back to a very important point on units and statistics.

You need to look *behind* the numbers. The majority of units sold are *new* units so the median figure is *predominantly made up of new prices*. If you tracked the percentage growth of a unit built and bought 20 years ago (as you would in the case of a house) you would find that it really only averaged 4 to 6 per cent growth. The statistics are effectively comparing oranges with lemons—and making lemons look good!

The fact is, a one-bedroom unit is just about the worst investment you can make (particularly if it's less than 50 m^2 in size). It scores low on capital growth (no land) and on leveraging ability: you can borrow between 90 and 100 per cent on a standard investment house in a capital city, but only 60 to 70 per cent on a unit (particularly a high-rise). In fact, a mortgage insurer requires a unit to have a minimum internal floor area of 50 m^2 (40 m^2 in some city metropolitan locations) for it to even be considered as security on a loan.

Forget the hype: four in five buyers are, over the long term, taking a loss on CBD units bought off the plan in Sydney and Melbourne. Why? Because only one in five people buy to live there: the rest are speculators who don't tend to look level-headedly at the real facts of supply and demand.

Yes, you will always find people who will advise you to buy units. 'Don't buy land,' they will say. 'You'll incur land tax; tenants don't like mowing lawns; it's easier to find tenants for units than for houses.'

> **Developers can make a healthy profit from selling units with nominal land value: is it any wonder they forget to mention that it's the *land* that appreciates?**

Look behind the veil. The fact is that developers can make a healthy profit from selling units with nominal land value: is it any wonder they forget to mention that it's the *land* that appreciates?

Land tax

'What about land tax?' you ask. Yes, it's a good question. While you will pay land tax, of course, it's not nearly as bad as people make out. The unimproved land value has to exceed a set threshold before you are charged land tax (this is calculated differently from state to state—see table S1.1, overleaf, for some examples). Table S1.2 (overleaf) lists the state thresholds—you can see, for example, that in Queensland the threshold is $599 999, which means you only pay tax on the land value in excess of that amount.

> *Land tax* is a state government tax calculated annually as a percentage of the Unimproved Capital Value (UCV). Each year the valuer general in each state values every block of land excluding any buildings on the land and any improvements. This is used for councils to calculate rates. The state government places a levy on all land owners (except for your principal place of residence—PPR). The annual tax is based on the total amount of land you own in that particular state. It's one reason why, if you're going to build a portfolio, it's not a bad idea to have land in two, three of four states, as I do.

Capital city	Median land price	Land tax
Sydney	$482 000	Nil
Melbourne	$290 000	$355
Brisbane	$272 000	Nil
Adelaide	$169 000	Nil
Perth	$230 000	Nil

Table S1.1: examples of land tax by capital city median house price

State	Threshold
New South Wales	$549 000
Victoria	$249 999
Queensland	$599 999
South Australia	$352 999
Western Australia	$299 999

Table S1.2: land tax thresholds by state

A cautionary tale

Dainford Limited developed thousands of high-rise units from 1970 to 1991, but it rarely held onto any because it found that they tended to lose their value.

This came home to me during the early 1980s when units dropped in value and one of my associates went on a buying rampage. He clinically offered just 60 to 65 per cent of the price that a unit had sold for less than three years earlier in nearly a dozen buildings across the Gold Coast. He held the units for 10 years and sold them again, averaging a 13.5 per cent per annum growth rate on his purchase price. He had the financial capacity to buy multiple units and to make cash offers to desperate vendors.

In hindsight, he could have achieved the same kind of growth—without having to deal with desperate vendors, and without taking a huge cash outflow on the chin—simply by buying *houses at market value*. (He would have done even better if he had bought *new* homes and claimed the depreciation as a tax-deductible item, as I'll discuss in Step 3.)

The real cautionary moral of the story, however, is the depreciating value of the units. My associate was able to buy them, second hand, at a capital *discount* of 30 to 40 per cent. It's almost like buying that new BMW Cabriolet and driving it out of the showroom knowing that as you cross over the grate its value is probably dropping by 20 to 30 per cent.

LAND APPRECIATES, BUILDINGS DEPRECIATE

Let me give you a 'land appreciates, buildings depreciate' story out of my own portfolio. I'll caution you by saying 'don't try this at home' because I wouldn't recommend it. During the heyday of 2006 I collected lots of 'work horses' (low-cost housing). I also had two beach houses at Fingal Beach just south of Tweed Heads in New South Wales, and decided to buy a third one in Byron Bay. I'd bought a 772 m² block of land with a very small (120 m²) house that was all but worthless and I had plans to renovate it. I paid $3 million and during the GFC it was a real weight on my portfolio as I had debt with the bank, which wanted to revalue it. At that time, it had probably gone down to $2.6 million (as trophy assets do), but in 2013–14 it finally began to go forward with the momentum from the Sydney cycle kicking in (Sydney median house prices had essentially been flat from 2003 to 2011 and then began appreciating rapidly from 2012 to 2017, doubling in value—that's a fairly typical cycle, though probably a bit elongated due to the GFC). I sold the property in 2017 for $7 million, which was solely land value as the purchaser intended to bulldoze the house. In real terms I paid $3886 per square metre for the land, and sold it for $9067 per square metre, which outperformed any median house price growth in that same period of time. The reason this wasn't ideal is because the banks wanted P&I repayments, which created real cash flow issues and slowed down my ability to duplicate my 'work horses' because of the impact of the negative valuation of $2.6 million. So, the take away, once again, is: land appreciates, buildings depreciate.

Does location matter?

Location is a *vital* factor in capital growth.

I recently ran a wealth-building workshop for high-income individuals in Melbourne. At the start of the workshop, half of them affirmed that they were already investing to build wealth. I asked what kinds of investment properties they had, and where. Answer: they were units, in and around inner residential Melbourne. I asked what the land content of those units was. Answer: a sea of confused faces.

> **You *have* to do some homework (or find someone to do it for you).**

These people—competent, clued-up people—had acquired units in the area where they lived purely on the basis that they would be easy to maintain and manage: a classic case of the 'I can drive by it on my way home from work' factor.

You *have* to do some homework (or find someone to do it for you).

DO YOUR HOMEWORK!

So many Australians invested in mining towns during the mining boom. If only they had read earlier copies of *7 Steps to Wealth*, they would have shied away from places such as Gladstone, Kalgoorlie, Bunbury, Mackay, Emerald and other towns that surged in population due to mining where I warned against investing. Such areas saw immediate profits because rental returns were good. One property sold to a residential investor at the heat of a mining boom for about $1.4 million based on the promise of crazy rental returns of up to 10 per cent. When the mining boom ended—as they always do—that property sold for $377000. That's the wrong way to start your portfolio. Do your homework: look for long-term sustained price growth, population growth and employment growth.

Where should you buy for capital growth?

The key factor is *demand*. And demand for residential property is underpinned by:

- estimated population growth
- employment opportunities
- lifestyle choices.

There are macro and micro factors involved here.

The *macro* factor is that the greatest growth of population and employment on an ongoing basis is concentrated in the capital cities. Figure S1.4 (overleaf) shows the actual population growth for the major capital cities over a 10-year period and figure S1.5 (overleaf) shows the projected population growth to 2050. Employment opportunities are also more abundant in the capital cities because they are home to established industries and industrial diversity (unlike regional areas, as we'll see a bit later). The *micro* point is that people—individuals and families—decide where they want to live.

Figure S1.4: annual population growth by capital city, 2006–16

Source: ABS Cat. No. 3218 'Regional Population Growth', http://www. abs.gov.au/AUSSTATS/abs@.nsf/mf/3218.0.

So when I'm building a portfolio, I base it on the factors that underpin demand as follows:

- *estimated population growth:* in 1991, there was an average of 2.65 people per household. The 2016 Australian Bureau of Statistics (ABS) census recorded an average of 2.59 people per household—which is not a rapid decline, albeit we do have a large number of single-tenant occupants (25 per cent).

The ABS has projected household size to continue to decline to 2.2–2.3 people per household by 2026, mainly due to the ageing population—although I would question these figures. Regardless, it is an urban myth that the average household size is currently 1–1.5 people.

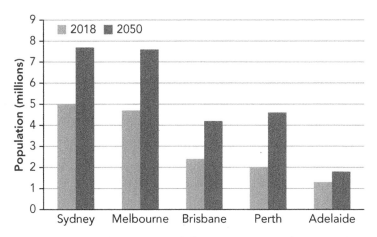

Figure S1.5: population growth forecast to 2050 by capital city

Source: ABS Cat. No. 3218 'Regional Population Growth', http://www.abs.
gov.au/AUSSTATS/abs@.nsf/mf/3218.0; http://www.abs.gov.au/ausstats/
abs@.nsf/mf/3222.0.

- *employment opportunities:* education and healthcare
  are huge employee sectors. Healthcare will employ 18.8
  per cent of all Australians in the next 10 to 15 years.
  Education is one of our fastest growing industries and
  our third largest export today, which coincides well
  with the need for immigration

- *lifestyle opportunities:* the Urban Land Institute
  identifies six main reasons why families with children
  live where they do:

  1. schools

  2. family security

  3. transport

  4. shops

  5. employment (healthcare and education)

  6. recreation.

Every single one of my investment properties is *within 5 kilometres* of (private) schools, shops and transport.

Every single one is in what I classify as a secure, family-oriented area: an area with a population as close as possible to three people per household, where at least seven out of 10 households are owner-occupiers—not investors. (You can get those statistics from the Australian Bureau of Statistics.)

How does this contribute to capital growth? If a suburb has three or more people per household and 60 per cent owner-occupation, there's going to be a strong demand for owner-occupied housing—and, often, their friends and family. With private schools nearby, they will tend to stay in the area for 10 to 20 years, depending on the age of their children. Owner-occupiers also tend to recapitalise their homes, and upgrade and maintain their grounds better than investors, making it a more attractive area to live in, injecting further demand—and capital—into the area.

And that's where another factor enters the picture.

The benchmark factor

The potential value of a property in any given area reflects the *best* or highest value of property in that area: this is called the 'established capital benchmark'.

When I buy an investment property, I look to buy in an area where I can pay substantially less than (maybe half or one-third of) the capital benchmark—that is, the price my neighbours paid to get into the area. This is what some people call 'the worst house in the best street': it represents great potential for immediate capital growth. I'd forsake some of my other location criteria to find this property.

Picture these two houses.

My house   My neighbour's house

The house on the right cost more than $300 000 to build on a $120 000 block of land in 1999: on completion it was worth $450 000/$500 000. (It sold in 2005 for $760 000.)

The house on the left is one of my investment properties. I paid $100 000 for my block of land and $107 000 for the house in 2001.

I invested $207 000 to be located next door to someone who had invested more than $400 000. Within 18 months, my property was revalued at more than $320 000.

That's great capital growth, thanks to the reflected value of the area as defined by the established capital benchmark—that is, the highest property price in the area. (Even better, I didn't put a cent of my own money into the house. In the first year, it cost me less than $2 per week—and thereafter, it was cash-flow positive! That's the beauty of my structure, as we'll see.)

If you want assured capital growth, buy in an area where there is a capital benchmark set by owner-occupiers who have been prepared to pay two or three times the price you will have to pay. That means a bit more homework on the internet—or perhaps driving around—but that's what effective real estate investment is all about.

What about regional areas?

As I noted earlier, the demand for property, confirmed by the 2016 ABS census, is likely to be strongest and most consistent in the main four capital cities.

Many investors buy into regional markets because they seem more affordable or they show better rental returns. But my experience has been that whenever there's a hiccup, it's those areas that are hit hardest. For example, when there is an economic downturn, unemployment figures can rise quickly—and with them, rental vacancy rates. That's one reason why banks aren't as bullish about offering 90- to 100-per-cent loans (high 'loan-value ratios') in those markets: another brake on your compound growth.

I have had experience in the regional markets of Gladstone, Coffs Harbour, Cairns and even as close to a capital city as the Gold Coast. I have also witnessed, first hand, the problems experienced in Canberra and Newcastle when a dominant local employer decides to relocate.

In a capital city, you have major industries feeding off each other, and a major population base that can attract new investment and further population growth.

If you are looking at building a property portfolio, you could be in a position—in 10 to 20 years' time—where you have accumulated 10 to 20 properties in a particular area. If a principal employer relocates or suffers financial strain (as with the government moving jobs out of Canberra, or BHP moving out of Newcastle), the area can free-fall into a downward spiral for anything up to 10 years. Geelong, in Victoria, is a regional market that suffered badly during 1990–91 due to the financial collapse of a major building society and the shut-down of manufacturing businesses: years later, the area hadn't yet bounced back, although the general property market in Melbourne had shown a solid recovery.

I live on the Gold Coast. I love the Gold Coast. I said in earlier editions of the book, however, that I classed it as a regional market, not as an area to build a significant portfolio. Well, I've had to revise my thinking, as the area has pushed through the 500 000 population barrier—and *still* has population growth forecasts that outperform all the mature cities (i.e. those with a population of more than 500 000).

There have been some significant updates to population growth forecasts since the 2016 ABS census that are relevant to building a property portfolio. The big picture is that Australia's population is ageing: nearly 25 per cent are baby boomers (born 1945–60) who will retire in 2010–30.

As I mentioned in chapter 2, government and business have recognised the need for skilled immigrants to replace retiring baby boomers and as a result, immigration is growing at record numbers. In 2008, Australia had its highest ever population growth on record of nearly 390 000, with skilled immigrants making up 230 000 of these (and 234 000 in 2016–17). The ABS is forecasting a population growth of more than 400 000 per annum until 2030, which means Australia's population will grow by nearly five million to around 30 million people!

Here is the other key point: of the five million population increase, nearly four million will move to the four main capital cities: Brisbane, Melbourne, Sydney and Perth. Adelaide has been the poor cousin with only about 20 per cent of what the other cities average. However, watch this space for the possible effects of Adelaide's focus on education and health care. Each of the other four capital cities mentioned above will increase in population by more than one million, except for Perth, which is tipped to increase by approximately 800 000—a significant number given the size of the city.

It reinforces what I wrote in the first edition of this book in 1997: *stick to the main capital cities.*

The GFC crystallised the shortage of housing accommodation in Australia, which was reaching crisis levels in 2005–07. At that time rents were rising by 10 to 15 per cent per annum in the main capital cities due to a housing supply shortage. Rental growth has now stabilised with the construction boom adding supply to housing since 2012.

We, at Custodian, along with thousands of our clients, have averaged 4 per cent rental growth per annum for the past 20 years despite various movements in interest rates, inflation and the GFC. It is a great cash flow position to be in.

Let's recap

- Land appreciates and buildings depreciate, so invest in a house/duplex with at least 30 per cent land content.

- Property appreciates with demand, so:

  » invest where population and jobs are growing

  » stay within a 45-minute drive of a capital city

  » purchase close to schools, family security, transport, shops, employment and recreation

  » buy below the median house price in an area with a high established capital benchmark.

- It's no wonder so many Australians retire on welfare when:

  » 29.5 per cent invest within their own postcode

  » 92 per cent buy second-hand properties

  » 50 per cent buy apartments

  » 34 per cent sell within five years of purchasing.

- By buying in a growth area, you not only maximise the capital growth on your property, you also have a high tenant population from which to generate rental income.

We'll talk about rent and renting in Step 2.

STEP 2
Optimise your income

The beauty of gearing and leveraging your investment property is that you can begin to build wealth with minimal capital by borrowing the balance of the acquisition costs of your investment property. The downside is that you have to service that debt. And then there are other outlays, such as maintenance and rates. The property doesn't pay for itself. Or does it? Residential property, as we've seen, has the potential to generate *income* to offset your cash outlays, while its capital value increases over time. Income is the fuel for capital growth. For 'income', read 'RENT'.

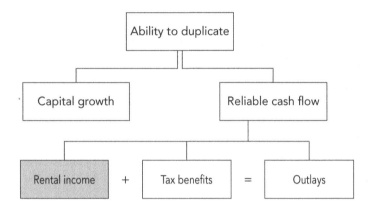

Who rents and why?

Ninety-five per cent of Australians have rented residential property at some time. More to the point, 30.9 per cent of Australians currently rent residential property (up from 26.9 per cent in 1991)—and the number seems to be increasing.

The number of older people, empty nesters, DINKS (double income, no kids) and single-parent families in our population is growing, and these categories tend to push up the demand for rental property (see figure S2.1). In addition, property price increases tend to outstrip inflation (which is great for capital growth) and therefore also outstrip rises in wages and salaries: the rental market grows as property prices gradually rise beyond the reach of more and more people.

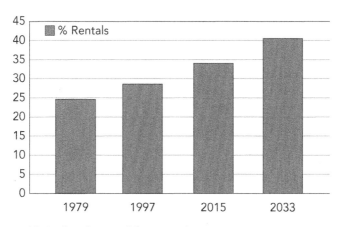

Figure S2.1: the demand for rental property

Source: ABS, and projected trend.

At the same time, the number of occupants per property is dropping, albeit slightly, but is expected to continue to drop (as shown in figure S2.2) in line with the increasing ageing population, as people over the age of 65 make up a large number of single-occupant households.

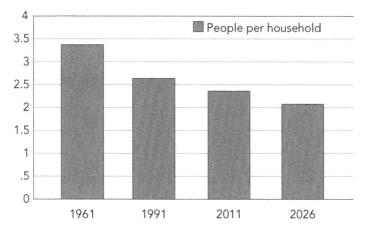

Figure S2.2: household size

Source: ABS, and projected trend.

So, we can safely project an increase in demand for rental property well into the 21st century.

> **We can safely project an increase in demand for rental property well into the 21st century.**

There are many advantages to renting—although, of course, capital growth isn't one of them! Flexibility is a major factor, in view of increasing mobility and decreasing job security. Not having financial or managerial responsibility for a property is attractive to many people. And, as we noted in chapter 1, a mortgage can seem like an unacceptable level of debt (if you don't look for the advantages of affordability, leverage and capital growth).

One important thing to recognise, however, is that your market for tenants is principally made up of people in the lower income bracket. This is where the demand is. And to take advantage of that demand, we need to buy properties that can be rented out at an affordable percentage of the average income. In other words, *aim for affordability* (see Step 5). We'll come back to this a bit later, when we discuss how much rent we should charge.

Optimising your rental income

Theoretically, there are two ways you could go about optimising your rental income:

- maximise your income by charging the highest possible rent. If you charge the highest possible rent on the cheapest possible property, your margins look particularly healthy (in theory)

- charge a moderate (even below-average) rent on a higher priced property in a more popular residential area.

If you wanted to be greedy, you might think the first option looks good ... and you'd be shooting yourself in the foot.

Optimising rental income does not mean charging the *highest* rent: it means ensuring that the property attracts and retains tenants, and therefore maintains a *constant* rental income. The key is avoiding *vacancy*, which generates no income at all.

The two biggest factors in avoiding vacancy are:

- *choosing the right area:* invest in an area with a high and preferably growing demand for rental property

- *charging affordable and competitive rents:* do your homework to establish how much rent you should be charging.

Let's take a look at these factors.

Choose the right area: beware 'bargains'

We'll tackle the most common mistake first: it's a false economy to buy into a secondary suburb (high unemployment, low property values) just because the property is 'cheap'. Property in a low-demand area may look like a bargain in purchase price terms, but it won't show a return in consistent rental income. (In property, a 'bargain' is just a way for someone to unload their problems onto you.)

We pinpointed Brisbane as a city currently showing significant population, employment and capital growth—and that's a step in the right direction, but you *still* need to do your

> **In property, a 'bargain' is just a way for someone to unload their problems onto you.**

homework. You could buy a house in some parts of Logan City, for example, for $400 000, and a unit for $300 000.

If that sounds like 'good value', look again: Logan City has double-digit unemployment figures, high youth crime rates and, not surprisingly, a lot of vacant property!

The area has tripped up a lot of property investors over the past 20 years. Developers and marketers have recklessly sold property that was grossly overvalued in parts of Woodridge and Kingston (Logan City), mainly to interstate buyers. For many years, those buyers had *negative* capital growth—and if they sold prior to the last boom, they would have suffered a significant loss. If they held on, they would finally have come out in front—but they would have been a lot better off if they had done a little homework! Meanwhile, they would also have been struggling with low rental demand and bearing the weekly cost of their borrowings—a cash flow nightmare.

This *doesn't* mean rental property isn't a good investment. On the contrary—and despite a few urban myths—the rental market is growing steadily, and many people who rent do so through choice, even in the lower income brackets. What it *does* mean is that you need to do your homework on the location and type of rental property that will attract and retain consistent, rent-paying tenants.

Where do families want to live?

Remember the six main reasons why people choose to live in a particular area:

1. proximity to schools
2. security (that is, safety) for the family
3. adequate public transport
4. proximity to shops
5. availability of (or proximity to) employment
6. recreational facilities.

These factors match my criteria for location for capital growth and my own survey of Brisbane rentals. They haven't changed at all over the past 30 years. In fact, they make pretty good sense and are a useful guide to the kind of residential area that sustains a high demand for rental property.

Choose a property where at least the top three of these six factors are present within a radius of, say, 3 kilometres: you'll not only be able to maintain a steady rental income, but you'll get capital growth as well.

Another factor is the *type* of property renters look for.

Even if you aren't thinking of resale values and capital growth based on land content (as discussed in Step 1), you'd want to think twice about buying units for rental. When you consider that only 6.1 per cent of Australians owner-occupy apartments, you might assume that everyone *rents* units. But the fact is that the *vacancy rate of units/townhouses is double that of houses in most areas*: in other words, more units lie empty and income-idle. Given affordability, the average Australian household of 2.6 people still prefers to live in detached housing.

Another tip: don't buy in *complexes* with multiple properties for sale to investors because:

- you will be competing against all the other investor-landlords for tenants

- owner-occupiers prefer to live in areas with fewer rental properties, so you will be limiting your property's onselling potential—and hence your capital growth. Invest in suburbs with no more than 35 per cent of homes occupied by renters. (Again, this weighs heavily against units, which are overwhelmingly renter-occupied.)

We've already mentioned, briefly, another good, practical yardstick for assessing the demand for rental property in a particular area: *vacancy factor*. Let's look at it in more detail.

Vacancy factor

The rental vacancy factor is the percentage of the total rental properties in a particular area that are vacant at any given time. It is a pretty fair reflection of demand for rental property in that area—and therefore a barometer of how consistent your rental income will be.

The easiest and most accurate way of determining the vacancy factor in an area you are interested in is to contact a couple of the local real estate agents and ask them:

- how many rental properties they have on their books (in total)
- how many of them are vacant at the moment.

Personally, I won't invest in an area where the rental vacancy factor is higher than 3 per cent. This needs to be reassessed on a suburb-by-suburb basis, as that vacancy factor from one city to another can vary from 1 to 20 per cent. So, once again, you have to do your homework.

Now, let me give you a word of caution in relation to the internet as a lot of people think they can do all their homework online: the internet can't be relied on for this kind of information. Agents often conveniently leave listings and rental properties on their websites even after they've sold or leased the property to attract buyers. So if you think you're doing all your homework by going on the internet, you're not. You're most likely being misled. Get on the phone, get in the car and go and see for yourself. Or, better still, visit the agent personally and ask them point blank what they have available for renting. Then go and see the properties yourself to find out whether they are actually rentable. As I've said before, do your homework—and not just on the internet.

Figure S2.3 shows the average rental vacancy rates across Australia.

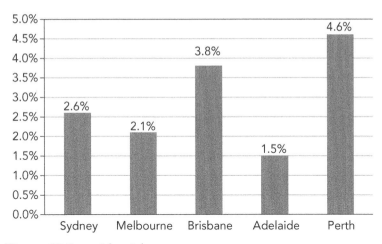

Figure S2.3: residential vacancy rates

Source: SQM Research, December 2017, https://propertyupdate.com.au/vacancy-rates-increase-in-most-cities-in-december/.

This is a useful exercise in interpreting available information. Data can give a false perspective on vacancy rates: the figures may include units *and* housing, disguising the risks and opportunities. For example, in Melbourne the vacancy rate for units could be 9 to 10 per cent, while housing may only be 1 to 2 per cent—risks in units, opportunities in houses. Similarly, you'll need to look at the position suburb by suburb: some are vastly over-supplied with rental properties, and so have much higher vacancy rates than others where there is still demand.

Charge affordable and competitive rents

If your property is empty, it is income-idle. If you want to maintain a constant income, you need to secure a constant supply of tenants. One good way of doing this is to check the suitability and vacancy factor of an area before you buy. Another is to avoid being greedy about rent.

Buy rental property on which the market rate of rent is *no more than 30 per cent of the average household's disposable income*. This makes it affordable to most people with a job. If disposable income is around $1500 per week, $500 per week is an affordable rent.

Table S2.1 shows the average incomes in the main capital cities. I use it as a barometer for buying and setting rent on properties. It's one of those 'changeable weather patterns' I mentioned in the introduction to this book, and requires ongoing monitoring as part of the basic discipline of wealth-building.

> **Even three weeks is a long time to have to pay the mortgage without the support of rental income.**

Over the years, I have made a point of renting my properties for about 5 per cent *below* the going market rate. That way, if I advertise a house on Saturday, by Sunday afternoon I will have it rented to the tenant of my choice. At a cost of just $10 to $15 per week, I have avoided having to compete with most other rental properties advertised, ensured minimal vacant time and had a number of applicants to choose from. Because I tend to acquire property at the low end of the range, my rents tend to be around $450 to $550 per week, which is highly affordable and attractive.

I see a lot of investors trying the opposite strategy: hanging out for the market rental value of their property—or more. For the sake of $10 or $20 per week, they may wait four to six weeks—during which time the property is vacant—and in the end, settle for any tenant who comes along, increasing the risk of rapid tenant turnover, or worse. Even three weeks is a long time to have to pay the mortgage without the support of rental income.

	Average weekly household income	Recommended affordable rental*
Sydney	$2395	$718
Melbourne	$2114	$634
Brisbane	$2160	$648
Adelaide	$1841	$552
Perth	$2413	$724

*Based on 30% of average weekly household income

Table S2.1: capital city rental affordability

Source: ABS 6523.0. Household Income and Income Distribution, Australia, 2011–12 report and RBA Inflation Calculator published by the ABS to adjust 2012 household disposable income to 2016.

The other temptation is for higher income earners to buy expensive properties and charge higher rents, thinking that since they have more money, they should invest in a higher priced property—surely it *must* be less of a hassle than having two smaller properties? Not necessarily—and this is not the best way to build wealth. (We'll discuss this in more detail in Step 5.)

In order for your income to pull its weight in offsetting your outlays—as our structure recommends—you will have to increase your rents from time to time in line with inflation. But if you set a discounted rental amount in the first place, and if you have invested in an area with high and growing rental demand, this shouldn't be a problem.

HOW MUCH RENT SHOULD YOU CHARGE?

In 1987–88, I acquired more than 30 rental properties in the regional town of Gladstone (south of Mackay), prior to a commitment by Queensland Government and Industry to more than $1 billion in capital works projects in the area. I spoke to a real estate agent about the total number of properties he had under management: more than 400 at the time, including the ones I had acquired. And he hardly had a vacancy.

I couldn't understand why the rents were hovering at $55 to $65 per week—and had been for the best part of six to seven years in a high-inflation environment. The agent's answer was that he couldn't justify a rent increase, and when I told him I was proposing to increase my tenants' rent, he swore flat out that they simply wouldn't pay it. I went ahead and increased the average rent from $65 per week to $120 per week and still did not have a single property vacant for more than two weeks at a time.

The moral of the story is: if you choose a high-demand, low-vacancy area, you will always have tenants, and, in my experience, you will be able to increase rents by 4.5 per cent per annum (or a percentage of the property's value) over the entire period of your ownership.

Post script: I got out of Gladstone in 1989. Remember the vulnerability of regional markets I talked about in Step 1? The promised investment in the city never came to fruition, and real estate prices remained flat there for the following nine years. Chalk it up as one of my mistakes.

The mining boom in 2007–12, and in particular liquefied natural gas, saw Gladstone have probably its biggest boom in history. Guess what happened at the end of it? … You guessed it: lots of disappointment. I even had people write to me saying they'd just bought in Gladstone and they'd read my book, but they felt things were different now because of the new liquefied natural gas industry — and they told themselves stories about how it would never happen again. Well guess what? Everything in property pretty much happens again!

Rental? But that means tenants!

This is another one of those areas where emotion tends to overtake logic. We've all heard the horror stories of bikie gangs inhabiting a property 10 people to a room, all but demolishing the house, never paying the rent, and leaving their luckless landlords with huge repair bills, a mortgage to service and eviction notices to draw up.

Okay, there are 'problem' tenants. (In fact, mostly there are 'tenants with problems', which is not quite the same thing.) Some problems can be avoided, and others can be overcome.

Let's look at some ways of avoiding problems with tenants.

✓ Set rents just below the market rate

This gives you greater discretion in choosing your tenants. It increases the likelihood that they will be able to continue to afford the rent. It also creates a degree of loyalty — and I find that tenants are more willing to look after the property and use their own initiative (and even money) to make small repairs and replacements knowing that their landlord is helping them out a little.

At the end of the day, $10 per week off your bottom-line income is a small price to pay for a comparatively hassle-free tenancy, particularly by the time you are the landlord of four or five properties.

✓ Check out prospective tenants the way you would a prospective employee

When the agents who manage one of my properties tell me that they have a new tenant for it, I want to know:

- Have they got a job, and how long have they been at that job? Does the employer back this up?

- Where have they lived for the past five years? Did they pay the rent? Was the bond refunded in full? Does the previous landlord back this up?

These two checks alone will weed out most potential bad tenants. You really do need to know the answer to these questions before you can rent a property—just like getting references from somebody you might consider employing. Potential good tenants won't mind being asked. You'll find a sample tenancy application form on page 167, if you're interested in the details.

✓ Cover the cost of the unexpected

People lose jobs, relationships break up, things happen.

Fortunately, there are insurance policies for almost everything, including some specifically tailored to rental properties. You can insure against financial loss—for example, by a tenant defaulting on rent or leaving without notice — if the outstanding amount is not already covered by the bond. You can also insure the building and its contents against accidental damage, fire, theft and malicious damage by the tenant. (The latter is actually pretty rare, despite the bikie gang stories!)

Do take out Landlord Protection Insurance. If you are buying a property for $500 000 — on which the rent might be $500 per week — it will cost you around $300 per year (that's less than a week's rent) to insure it. This will ensure that you receive a full 52 weeks' rent per year. In fact, we insist that all Custodian clients take out such insurance. That way, if a tenant leaves without paying the rent or causes malicious damage, the necessary bills can still be paid. It is absolutely vital to your wealth-building program that you *maintain your cash flow*: you can't afford to be late with interest payments because banks charge penalties — which are sometimes 3 to 4 per cent above their going rate.

I also set aside a contingency fund of two months' rent, plus the amount of the excess payable on any insurance claim. That's usually enough to give everybody some leeway.

BE PREPARED FOR THE WORST

Some time ago, I rented a property to a nice young couple, both with jobs. They were in a de facto relationship that had lasted for two years. Their jobs checked out, and the bond from their previous rental had been refunded in full. So far, so good. Unfortunately, the relationship hit the rocks: she moved out, he lost it, and then he lost his job... Six weeks later (after I had evicted him), I found that he had used the ceiling in the third bedroom as an elaborate watering system for growing marijuana. The insurance covered $610. However, I had to fork out the money for repairs before the insurance company paid up, mainly so I could rent the property out again quickly. My policy didn't cover loss of rent (in those days, I didn't worry about such things, but if I had had the kind of policy I have now at the time, the excess would only have been about $160 ... you live and learn!) As it was, the net cost to me was around $860 ($2500 in today's terms): about five weeks' rent.

If things can happen, they will—and usually all at the same time!

In light of this story, my formula of two months' rent plus rental insurance excess may seem overly cautious, but if you are building a portfolio of five or six properties, it's best to operate under Murphy's Law: if things can happen, they will—and usually all at the same time!

✓ Get someone else to take on the management tasks— and hassles—for you

A professional managing agent can take everything out of your hands (if that's what you want): advertise the property; vet and select tenants; organise maintenance; handle finance; communicate with the tenants, local authorities and service providers; and so on. (In appendix A, I've reproduced the form we use to ensure that agents vet our tenants effectively.)

Don't just give the property management to *any* agent. As always, look behind the veil. Make sure the agent is well established: a full-time property manager and a large rent roll with few vacancies are good signs. Ask the agent for a reference from some of the landlords they work for. And please don't fall into the trap of going with the agent who offers you the most rent! Remember, higher rent can mean more hassles and longer vacancies.

Let's recap

- Beware of bargains—they are a way for people to unload their problems onto you.

- Charge slightly under the going rental rate to ensure your property is always rented.

- Rents rise by 4 to 5 per cent per annum. That's better than wage growth.

- Location is important. Make sure you buy where there is going to be constant and growing demand.

- Check out your tenants.

- Don't let words like 'problem', 'insurance' and 'eviction' put you off! Managing tenants is seldom as much of a hassle as you might fear—even if you choose to handle it yourself. And income from rent is the fuel for your capital growth.

- And remember: *do your homework*!

Rental income on its own will not cover all your outlays on an investment property. But there's another source of income available from your investment property: paying less tax!

We'll talk about the tax benefits of investment properties in Step 3.

Maximise your tax benefits

Along with earning income, saving tax is an essential 'fuel' for building wealth. As we saw in chapter 3, maximising your tax benefits is fundamental to the '7 steps to wealth' structure. This will ensure you have minimal cash outlays on your investment property, which will avoid significant restrictions on your ability to build your portfolio by reinvesting your increased equity.

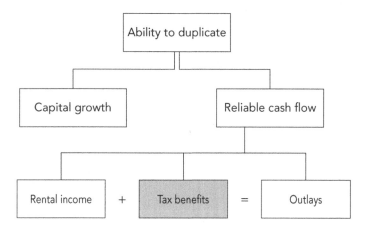

This — at last! — is where 'negative gearing' comes in.

What is negative gearing?

'Gearing' is borrowing money for the purposes of investment — and we will be discussing how to get the most out of it in Step 4 by obtaining and using finance.

'Negative gearing' is the tax benefit that accrues when the income from an investment fails to cover the outlays on that investment so that you are making a 'book loss', or negative income. (Don't panic: remember, the capital value of your asset is still growing.) A residential investment property would be negatively geared if, for example, the mortgage interest and other tax-deductible items exceeded the rental income.

> *Negative gearing* occurs when your total outlays to maintain an investment are greater than your income from the investment: the difference is claimable as a tax deduction.

The thing is, this loss—the difference between your outlays and your income—is *tax deductible*. It can be offset against your personal income (including salary) to reduce your taxable income, and perhaps even put you in a lower tax bracket. The upshot is that you *pay less tax*—and if that doesn't sound like a good idea, there's something pretty unusual about your thinking.

What deductions can you claim?

Here are some of the main cash deductions you can claim on any rental property:

- ✓ *loan interest* (other borrowing costs—such as loan application and valuation fees, mortgage registration and insurance—are deductible over a period of time)
- ✓ *insurance premiums*
- ✓ *fees*—for example, for property/rental management, legal advice and accountancy (if you decide to get all these deductions drawn up by a professional; you could also pay your spouse a fee for keeping regular accounts on the property, and claim that, which may reduce your combined income tax bill)
- ✓ *rates and local government charges*
- ✓ *maintenance, repairs and upkeep costs*
- ✓ *sundry business expenses* such as bank charges, stationery and travel (including reasonable inspections of property out of state).

Here's an example of the deductions you could claim on a second-hand investment property.

EXAMPLE 1: DEDUCTIONS ON A SECOND-HAND INVESTMENT PROPERTY

Say you purchase a rental property for $500000, borrowing 90 per cent of the purchase price at 7 per cent (interest only), and you let it out at $500 per week for 50 weeks of the year, for an annual rental income of $25000.

	$	
Rental income		$25000
Deductions:	$	
Loan interest	31500	
Insurance	1000	
Maintenance	200	
Rates	1800	
Rental management	2200	
Total annual cash outlay	36700	
Borrowing costs	400	
Total deductions	(37100)	
Shortfall		$12100

That shortfall is deducted from your gross income. So if your income is, say, $75000, your taxable income would be $62900. Here's the basic calculation based on one tax year:

	After deductions on property:	
Gross income: $75000	Taxable income:	$62900
Tax payable: $17422	Tax payable:	$13247
Net after-tax	Net after-tax	
income: $57578	income:	$49653
	Tax saving:	$4175

Example 1 was based on buying an older property, as 77 per cent of investors who take advantage of negative gearing do. It doesn't offer much of a tax deduction, but it is a negatively geared asset, so you do get a tax saving.

The difference that makes a difference: depreciation

Let me start by saying that 90 per cent of investors buy second-hand property. That's a mistake. It's a mistake because the golden rule of real estate is that 'land appreciates, buildings depreciate' so they're essentially buying buildings that are depreciating and are therefore not getting a tax deduction. The difference is that if you buy new buildings you can obtain a tax deduction. (As a side note, you can buy older buildings and claim a tax deduction but you need a quantity surveyor's report and the older the building, the fewer the deductions you can make—but you can't claim any deductions for anything built after 1987.) So, I stick with new buildings. Added to this, the federal Labor party—which isn't in government as I write but eventually will be—is going to outlaw negative gearing on all second-hand properties.

The *depreciation of an asset used to produce income* is a non-cash deductible item. This means you can claim a percentage of the declining value of items such as furniture, fixtures and fittings over a number of years of wear and tear. But somewhere in that list of depreciating items—such as carpets, curtains, cupboards and cookers—is the biggest item of all: the building.

Here's the key: a residential building constructed after July 1985 that is used to produce income can be depreciated (see Table S3.1).

Construction commenced	Claimable depreciation rate p/a	Over
18 July 1985–15 September 1987	4%	25 years
16 September 1987 onwards	2.5%	40 years

Table S3.1: rates of depreciation for residential buildings constructed after 1985

Depreciation on a new building can add up to thousands of dollars a year—and it's a 'non-cash' deduction, which means you don't actually have to lay out any cash each year in order to claim the 'loss'. This is the factor that significantly reduces your taxable income—and your tax payments. It's what makes our *income + tax benefits − outlays* structure work best.

Let's see how example 1 would look if you bought a *new* rental property of the same value and on the same terms.

EXAMPLE 2: DEPRECIATION ON A NEW INVESTMENT PROPERTY

Rental income		$25 000
	$	
Total annual cash outlay	36 700	
Non-cash costs:		
Borrowing costs	400	
Depreciation	9 000	
Total deductions	(46 100)	
Shortfall		$21 100

Your taxable income is now ($75 000 − $21 100) = $53 900.

And here's the new tax calculation:

After deductions on new property:

Gross income: Taxable income:

       $75 000 $53 900

Tax payable: $17 422   Tax payable: $10 142

Net after-tax   Net after-tax

    Income: $57 578   Income: $43 758

Your tax has been reduced by $7280.

And if you think of it purely in cash flow terms:

Investment Cash Flow

Rental income	$25 000 per annum
Cash outlays	($36 700) per annum
Cash shortfall	($11 700) per annum
Tax benefit (after non-cash deductions)	$7 280 per annum
After tax cost	$4 420
Cost per week:	$85.00

This allows you an earlier opportunity to add on to your portfolio without eating into your personal cash flow too much. And our example only shows one property: try multiplying the effect by five or six! And please note I have used 7 per cent as the interest rate rather than the current 5 per cent rate.

It's all about *cash flow management*. You've got the opportunity to write off the construction value of the house and fittings over several years, leaving only the bare land value, which is the part of your investment that's going to go up in value. The components of your house-and-land package should look something like this:

Total purchase price	$500 000
Land	$250 000
House (structure)	$230 000
Fittings	$20 000

You can write off the fittings over the first five years, which is a major boost to your income and to your ability to add on to your portfolio during that period. That's efficient cash flow management and wealth-building.

In order to maximise your depreciation, you'll need a quantity surveyor's report. A lot of investors and even accountants think depreciation is 2.5 per cent of the value of the building. In fact, if the building is new, you can get a quantity surveyor to separate the fixtures and fittings from the building structure and claim 'accelerated depreciation'—potentially 10 to 20 per cent per annum—on the fixtures and fittings. This offers a useful additional cash flow for your first five years of ownership, until your rent grows to the point where you become cash flow positive. It's a completely legitimate 'trick' of the trade that all investors should be taking advantage of.

Who wants to pay more tax than they have to?

I know the maths can be a bit mind boggling, but it's not essential to do all the sums at this stage. (Once you get into negatively geared investments, it's a good idea, in any case, to have your tax return completed by a competent accountant or tax adviser so that you're sure to claim all your legitimate deductions.)

But here's the bottom line. Am I really saying that by claiming a 'book loss' you can not only cover the shortfall, but actually walk away with extra cash in your pay packet? That's exactly what I'm saying.

At the moment, if you're on a salary of, say, $100000, you may have to work Monday and part of Tuesday of each week *just to pay the tax!*

> **Am I saying that you can actually walk away with extra cash in your pay packet? That's exactly what I'm saying.**

Negative gearing allows you to legitimately minimise the amount of tax you pay as well as fuelling capital growth. Negatively geared rental property is one of the most tax-efficient investment vehicles available. And yet, only 3 per cent of Australians maximise their tax benefits.

If you are a PAYG income tax payer, and your deductions are more than $500 or 10 per cent of your gross salary (whichever

> **Only 3 per cent of Australians maximise their tax benefits.**

is greater) for the year, you don't even have to wait for an end-of-year refund: you can claim an immediate adjustment to the tax that is deducted from your salary by your employer. Section 15-15 (Schedule 1) of the *Tax Administration Act 1953* provides for this PAYG income tax withholding adjustment and the form used to claim for it is called a PAYG Income Tax Withholding Variation (ITWV).

Anybody on PAYG income ought to look into this! The higher your income and your marginal tax rate, the more tax you can save.

Need any further incentives?

There is also a little gem hidden in the fine print of the *Income Tax Administration Act 1997* that can improve your bottom line. Under Section 8.1, you may be able to claim payment of a reasonable sum (reflecting time and effort spent) to your spouse, a friend or another nominated person as a fee for managing the books of your rental property. (We call this 'grocery money'.) This may reduce the combined tax bill of the individuals.

Positive thinking for negative gearing

Quite simply, if you buy a house built before 1985 as an investment property, you need your head read! Why would you do it?

> **This isn't your home we're talking about; it's a negatively geared asset.**

A lot of investors acquire older properties because they think they're 'better value' (e.g. they can save an extra $5000 or $10000 on the purchase price) or perhaps they 'prefer the feel' of an older house. But—at the risk of repeating myself—it is the *land* that appreciates in value: the house is only the vehicle for generating rental income and qualifying for tax deductions so that you can offset your cash outlays while you achieve capital growth.

It really doesn't matter if you pay a bit extra for a newer property: it will more than pay for itself via a substantial tax rebate. And it *really* doesn't matter if you 'like' an old house: this isn't your home we're talking about; it's a negatively geared asset for offsetting your tax and maximising your income. Logic—not emotion—is needed for capital growth.

Remember our structure (in chapter 3): that's what cash flow management and negative gearing are all about. Figure S3.1 demonstrates how the outlays are broken down using the figures from example 2.

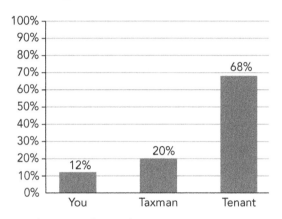

Figure S3.1: who pays the outlays?

Table S3.2 shows the real value of buying new versus buying old.

	New (newly built house)	Old (5-year-old house)
Price	$500 000	$475 000
Land value	$250 000	$250 000
Building	$250 000	$225 000
Depreciable amount	$250 000	$197 000
'Real' purchase price (for the land)	$250 000	$278 000

Table S3.2: buying new vs buying old

Let's say you find a new house priced at $500 000 and a five-year-old (otherwise comparable) house next door for sale at $475 000. Most investors would buy the five-year-old house thinking it was a better investment—perhaps even jumping to the conclusion that they had found the 'worst house in the best street'.

But look beneath the surface of the asset: what is its real, depreciable value to you? In the case of the brand new home, you can write off the total amount of the building, so you're effectively paying what the key asset (the land) is really worth. In the case of the five-year-old home, you can only write off perhaps 85 per cent of the building value, leaving you paying more than the land's true value.

Depreciation is a key factor that will help you identify the intrinsic value of a property asset—in other words, the value of the *land*, since that's the commodity that is going to appreciate in value.

The money pit

One thing I have purposefully not mentioned in my comparative calculations above is the 'surprise' maintenance costs of older properties. Older properties have lots of hidden issues previous owners may have 'glossed over'. It's a major problem because house maintenance can be very expensive. I buy new and I get a guarantee from the builder on any structural maintenance costs for 10 years. If you are buying older properties you should allow 5 per cent of the replacement cost of the house each year as cash for maintenance. One of my mentors once told me, 'Cash is like oxygen: if you run out it will be over for you very quickly. Don't take the risk'.

Food for thought?

Let's recap

- Tax is your secret weapon to effective cash flow, particularly with the added bonus of depreciation.

- Avoid older properties as the deductions are less and the cash flow is much harder to forecast.

- You can claim your tax deduction for your property immediately and receive it in your fortnightly pay rather than wait until the end of the year.

Next, we're going to learn about step 4 of the 7 steps to wealth: using finance to build wealth.

Finance to build wealth

In chapter 3, we saw that building a residential investment real estate portfolio is based on gearing and leveraging so that you can:

- minimise your initial capital input into the investment (10 per cent equity)
- use the bank's money—in effect—to build wealth (90 per cent borrowing)
- reap a 100 per cent per annum return on your capital
- offset your costs with rental income and the tax benefits of negative gearing
- use equity growth to provide start-up equity for subsequent acquisitions by duplicating the process.

I trust that, by now, all that sounds pretty straight forward! (If it doesn't, don't worry. Really. As you investigate further—and still more as you begin to work the system—it will all fall into place.)

In this step, we will look at some of the practical issues around gearing: property values and valuations, choosing and using loan providers, and evaluating different finance options.

Assessing the value of property

It's vital that you're able to make a basic assessment of the value of a property so you can check that you're paying a fair price.

The key to the valuation—and capital growth—of your property will (as ever) be the land.

One simple method of determining the value of your investment is to divide it into two components: the land value and the replacement cost of the building.

For a house, this is quite simple: you can usually estimate the land value by sales of comparable vacant land sites.

This information can be obtained from the valuer general's office in the appropriate state department. (For example, in Queensland, it is the Department of Environment and Resource Management; in New South Wales, it is the Land and Property Management Authority; in Victoria, it is the Department of Sustainability and Environment; and in Western Australia, it is the Department of Commerce.) You just have to request a sales report of all residential allotments within a recent period. (Alternatively, rates notices include 'unimproved land values'.) Another easy method is to ask the real estate agent or developer about the land component of a property. In a new estate, this is pretty straight forward, and you should also get some forecasts of future development and projected land values as an indication of how your equity might increase over time.

The other component is the replacement cost of the house. You can estimate this by using a simple formula:

total size of house (square metres) × $ rate per square metre

Builders aren't always eager to give out rates per square metre, but in most capital cities you can find project homes advertised in the newspapers with a reasonable range of standard building rates, usually from $1000 to $1500 per square metre. This doesn't include footings, so add on another $100 per square metre for footings and earthworks, and then have a quantity surveyor identify the value of your fixtures and fittings, as well as landscaping. (In any case, it's a good idea to get a quantity surveyor's valuation when you are claiming tax deductions for depreciation, as discussed in Step 3—and for a cost of $400 to $500, this is a useful cross-check.)

The other method of assessing a property's value is by simply looking at comparable sales. However, this is an inaccurate approach at best, and can be deceptive. You don't know the purchaser's or vendor's circumstances, which may have distorted the price. In the case of blocks of units, they may have been sold with incentives—or to non-resident owners who didn't bother to check out the value beneath the price tag—with the result that few owners have actually paid anything resembling replacement cost. I prefer to do a search with the relevant state's valuer general's office, checking sales over the previous six months where the purchaser's address coincides with the property sold—that is, where the owner is a resident.

Bank valuations

The dynamic of equity growth (using interest-only loans) is that the debt stays constant, while the value of the property goes up. But who defines the 'value' part of that equation?

For the purposes of assessing equity, the only valuation that matters is the one adopted by the bank that is lending you the balance of the acquisition costs.

Ideally, the value used by your lender should be the same as the purchase price, or more.

Ideally, the value used by your lender should be the same as the purchase price, or more.

If the bank valuation is significantly lower than the purchase price (and therefore the amount of the loan), the bank may protect itself by appraising the property at less than what you paid—and this can affect your total equity position with that bank. Unfortunately, this is not a rare occurrence; bank valuations can be deceptive—and potentially disastrous.

Here's an example showing how vital it is that the bank values your property in your favour.

THE IMPORTANCE OF GETTING THE RIGHT BANK VALUATION

Let's say your home is worth $800 000 and you have a debt with the bank of $300 000.

You apply to buy a new investment property priced at $500 000. You use the equity from your home and roll the loans together into a single loan package, which enables you to borrow 100 per cent of the purchase price and all the costs. (This is called *zero-cost financing* and we'll discuss it in more detail later.) However, the bank's valuation of your investment property—undisclosed to you—is only $400 000. Here's what happens.

Own home house value:	$800 000
Amount borrowed:	$300 000
Equity:	$500 000 (62.5%)
Investment property purchase price:	$500 000
Costs:	$20 000
Total amount borrowed:	$520 000
Bank valuation:	$400 000
Total security value of assets (house value + bank's valuation of investment property):	$1.2 million
Total borrowings:	$820 000
Equity:	$380 000 (32%)

Your equity has plunged from 62.5 per cent to 32 per cent, and your net assets from $500 000 to $380 000 according to the bank.

And you're not unique: this happens depressingly often.

People purchase all types of investment property — from high-rise units to townhouse units and houses — at overinflated prices: anything from $30000 to $100000 over the bank's appraisal of the property's security value.

Bank valuations can be deceptive — and potentially disastrous. Frankly, I think it's outrageous that banks continue to undervalue the investment property and not fully disclose this undervaluation to you as the borrower when they write your loan. If they aren't prepared to disclose their valuer's appraisal of the security value of the investment property, their loan should be limited to the amount of their valuation. It could take investors five to 10 years to recoup their lost capital as a result of a wide differential!

Caveat emptor: buyer beware

To ensure you don't get caught out on this:

- *avoid cross-collateralisation.* This is when lenders use all properties mortgaged as security for your outstanding loans. You need to find a lender who will advance the highest proportion of the property's purchase (a high loan-to-value ratio, or LVR) *without* requiring the use of *another* property — or the family home — as additional collateral. In other words, take out a separate loan for your investment property

- *watch out for 'all monies' clauses.* These allow lenders to secure 'any' outstanding loans you have with them (home loan, credit card, personal loan, overdraft and so on) against the value of the mortgaged property, whether they have advised you of this directly or not.

This may mean financing your investment property with a *different lender* from the one that holds the mortgage on the family home and other accounts, and it gives you added protection, should there be a problem with your investment portfolio (or your own credit cards) at any time, since your home isn't tied up with your investment.

You can still use the equity in your own home effectively by simply applying to your home-loan bank for the 10 per cent deposit on your first investment property.

In any case, find a lender who is prepared to disclose the security value of the property you are acquiring. If you are acquiring it through an agent and using a finance broker, obtain a copy of the valuation. Ensure that it equals your purchase price or comes within, say, 5 per cent of it. (I must admit that I have often had to settle for an assessment that didn't quite meet my price. Read on, and you'll find out why.)

Valuers

Given that it is the bank's perception of the value of the property that matters, you'd hope to be able to have confidence in the people they get to do the valuations. Nice thought.

Banks will often instruct panel valuers to value the property, and some of the most frustrating experiences I've had in real-estate investment over the years have been dealings with these self-styled 'experts' in property. Valuations are not, at the best of times, an exact science. The banks use valuers because they have an insurance indemnity: if an investor defaults and it is found that the property valuation was not representative of market values at the time of purchase, the bank can claim against the valuer.

> **Given that it is the bank's perception of the value of the property that matters, you'd hope to be able to have confidence in the people they get to do the valuations. Nice thought.**

I have seen a property valued by three different valuers where the highest valuation was double the lowest!

The big valuation firms tend to have young valuers—often in their twenties—doing 10 to 15 valuations a day, which doesn't allow time for painstaking research. They will search an area through the Valuer General's office and find a benchmark, or range of sales. The Valuer General's sales records are three to six months old, so if the market is really moving, it may not be reflected in the valuation. Moreover, valuers will often use the *lowest* comparable sale price for your purchase because their instructions from the bank are to supply a value at which the property would sell in the local market within three months. (This may vary if you have been required to take out mortgage insurance.)

Valuers will quite openly admit that if they were valuing a property for *you*—as opposed to the bank—they might strike a higher valuation figure. As it is, they are bound to be conservative.

So the valuation may well be a little under your price, but anything more than 5 per cent under is a worry. Don't forget: this is the basis of the bank's assessment of your net equity!

Once again: do the homework (preferably, yourself). Find comparable sales to *locals*—not out-of-state speculators—and if you can't, *don't buy*.

The point is: don't expect too much from valuers, but remember that the banks will rely on them. You need to work with them in order to secure equity growth and build a property portfolio. It's a good idea to:

- establish a relationship with the bank-appointed valuer yourself, so you understand their methodology in carrying out the initial valuation of a property. Don't be afraid to argue the point. As I mentioned above, most busy valuers are *so* busy that they tend to be conservative, but I've also seen them accept good, up-to-date evidence and change their initial appraisal

- ask the valuer to revisit your property if you become aware that there may have been some increase in the value of comparable properties; and on a six- to 12-month basis.

If you are going to appoint your own valuer, check that they will be acceptable to your bank. This way, you have access to the valuation information and you know that this valuer's appraisal will be accepted by the bank.

Choosing a loan provider

Selecting the right source of finance for your investment portfolio is integral to your capacity to build wealth.

This is another one of those decisions that needs to be made on logic, not emotion. Don't get sentimental about banks. Don't feel you have to be loyal to a bank (even if it's a big-name lender, it sponsors your favourite sporting event, it already holds your account or home loan, and the staff at your local branch are friendly!). With banks, loyalty only goes one way: they are uncaring at best—and at worst, they can be incompetent or manipulative, or both.

Remember our muscle-building analogy in chapter 3? If finance corresponds to the carbohydrates that fuel your exercise, the lender is merely the brand of cereal or bread you choose to provide those carbohydrates. If you don't like the flavour of one, switch to another. Fortunately, competition is increasing within—and from outside—the bank sector, and you should be able to find a lender willing to accommodate you if you shop around.

Don't get sentimental about banks.

So what is a logical way of selecting and dealing with a loan provider? Here are a few of the major considerations.

- You need to establish with the bank from the outset that you intend to use the increased equity in the property to build an investment portfolio. Most of the important questions and decisions flow from there.

- Banks lend against security. You need to know the bank's loan-to-value ratio (LVR)—that is, what percentage it will lend on investment properties. Some banks only lend 60 per cent of the valuation (or contract price), and others lend up to 90 per cent. You are looking for a bank that will accept a 10 per cent equity position because, under our structure, most of your outlays are being met, so you can afford to borrow 90 per cent and then, as soon as your first property increases in value by 10 per cent, you should have enough equity with that bank to acquire a second property (and so on). If a bank requires 20 per cent equity, it will take you twice as long to build a portfolio with that particular bank.

Also, be aware that, over time, the bank may move the goal posts on their lending criteria. This may be your signal to change banks.

So remember:

- find a lender who will give you a high LVR *without cross-collateralisation*—that is, without requiring the use of another property (e.g. the family home) as additional security. This protects your equity in other properties if there is a problem with one

- for a loan of more than 80 per cent, you will be required to take out *mortgage insurance* to cover the lender against potential losses if you default. (This is a once-only payment, and is tax deductible over a period of time.) The main insurers—Genworth and QBE—may call for an independent valuation, so it is a good idea to ensure that the bank's valuer is on the mortgage valuation panel as well

- banks also lend against your anticipated ability to service the debt—that is, to maintain repayments. The *affordability* of the loan is calculated by total repayments (of all loans, credit card debts and so on) as a percentage of your gross income. Most banks are comfortable with 30 to 35 per cent, but the figure can go as low as 25 per cent and as high as 60 per cent so shop around. I look for a bank that will do 40 per cent

- aim for 80 per cent of the projected rental income from the investment property to be included in your income for credit assessment, and for the *tax savings on negative gearing to be taken into account*: banks calculate this in different ways, and it can greatly impact how much you can borrow

- the bank must be prepared to *disclose its appraisal of the security value* of the property for comparison with the purchase price

- check for unnecessary or hidden *fees*: loan application fees, valuation fees, penalties for paying out early (including refinancing), administration charges and so on

- the bank must be flexible about *revisiting valuations*. Property, roughly speaking, doubles in value every eight to 10 years, but within that trend there are constant fluctuations: you need to be checking comparable sales for signs of rising values and the increased equity that you can use to increase your portfolio. Some of the major banks are less inclined to consider a revised valuation within 12 months of acquisition

- consider the effect of 'all monies' clauses: you may want to finance your investment property with a different lender from the one who holds your other accounts.

Table S4.1 is a compilation of investment banks, what they will lend and options for building a portfolio.

As you can see, none of the banks currently disclose valuations and they have no policy on revisiting valuations inside of 12 months. You will need to monitor such policies, and push for their relaxation, if you are going to make the structure work—and you will find more flexibility among second-tier banks than among the big four.

Loans are also available from some of the major insurance companies and credit unions, or through a mortgage broker (for a fee)—but frankly, it is the second-tier banks that are going to be most useful to you in building your property portfolio. Again, shop around. It may be worth paying an extra 0.25 to 0.50 per cent in interest to find a lender who is prepared to support you in building a portfolio over time.

Be prepared to negotiate the interest rate. Indicate your intentions and ask questions. You may be able to obtain pre-approval at the time of your first acquisition.

Bank	Application fee	Annual ongoing fee	Mortgage insurance fee as % of loan	LVR	Value disclosure	Revalue in 12 months
Westpac	$600	$96	2.16	90	no	No policy
CBA	$800	$96	2.13	90	no*	No policy
ANZ	$600	$60	2.13	90	no	No policy
St George	$700	$144	2.16	90	no	No policy
Suncorp	$600	$120	2.13	90	no	No policy
NAB	$600	$96	2.13	90	no	No policy

*Yes—if valuation ordered by broker Based on scenario of $500 000 loan.

Results may vary as each deal is assessed on a case-by-case basis.

Table S4.1: major financial institutions' lending guidelines

Source: Westpac, CBA, ANZ, St George, Suncorp, NAB, 2018.

Using a broker

There are some big advantages in using a finance broker to shop around for a deal for you. A major broker can often get you a better deal with your own bank than you could. (Sad, isn't it?) Some of these brokers are doing $100 to $200 million worth of financing per month—and the banks are happy to pay them commissions and trail fees (a percentage of your interest for the life of the loan) in order to secure the business.

Your first port of call may well be your local bank manager (who after all has probably been knocking on your door wanting to lend you money). But if you are using your home as part of the equity, it could be harder than pulling sharks' teeth to get your home mortgage released from your investment portfolio (which has got to be your short-term goal). Local bank managers tend not to like this idea because their security is better served by holding the deed to your home, but a broker has the negotiating power to represent *your* interests.

> **A major broker can often get you a better deal with your own bank than you could. (Sad, isn't it?)**

Some of the smaller brokers charge a fee for their service, but if you are going to use a broker, I would in any case recommend one of the larger ones, who have got the turnover—and therefore the negotiating power—to get you the best deal. Test them out and get them to offer you financing through a couple of banks on the terms and conditions you want—including having the valuation disclosed and the option to use equity in six to 12 months to repurchase.

Ten years ago, I set up Investloan, my own brokerage business, because I was frustrated with the banks and I couldn't find a broker to represent my interests. You can check them out if you're not getting anywhere with your bank or broker (www.investloan.com.au).

Choosing a finance option

Your finance options should be fairly simple: pay principle and interest (P&I) or interest only (IO). As an investor, however, the question also arises of whether you should invest your own cash or save your cash and use the equity in your home. Let's discuss the options.

Zero-cost financing

This is really just a fancy term for using the equity in your own home as collateral security for your investment property, instead of having to find a cash deposit. (We gave one example of how this can be done earlier to emphasise that the bank's valuation must be the same as the purchase price.) This can be highly tax effective as all the costs of acquiring your *investment* property, as well as the interest costs of the loan, can be deducted from your income tax. The repayments on your *home* are not similarly tax deductible. So if you do have spare cash, you are far better off using it to pay off your existing home mortgage and, in effect, using the equity it generates to borrow 100 or even 110 per cent on your investment property! Let's look at some numbers.

Home value:	$800 000
Outstanding debt:	$300 000
Value of investment property:	$500 000
Stamp duty, legal/finance costs, etc.:	$20 000
Total acquisition costs:	$520 000
Total assets (bank's valuation):	$1 200 000
Total debt:	$820 000
Of which:	
Investment debt (tax deductible):	$520 000

Your goal should be to try to divert as much of your taxable income into your wealth-building program as possible — using all legal opportunities available to you — in order to minimise your tax.

Interest-only loans

Maximum tax deductions are based on interest-only loans, as opposed to principal and interest (P&I) loans, because only *interest* payments are tax deductible.

Banks aren't always enthusiastic about interest-only loans as they prefer some principal to be paid off, but as you've probably realised by now, wealth-building is about *managing your cash flow*: where you have an opportunity to minimise your cash outlays, do it. This will allow you to build earlier. (If you have any spare cash, use it to pay off the principal on your home loan.)

If you took out a P&I loan for $150 000 over 25 years at an interest rate of 7 per cent, in the first five years you would repay $13 257, or about 9 per cent of the loan. This would affect your cash flow by $51 per week (in after-tax dollars). It's also money that could otherwise have been ploughed back into wealth-building.

Locking in an interest rate

The most important thing in wealth-building (if I may say it just one more time) is to manage your cash flow, not to get the highest rent, *nor the lowest interest rate*. My advice is to lock in your loan at the best rate you can find, for as long as you can.

You don't have to be in the business of interest rate forecasting to do this, although there are hundreds of economists and pseudo-economists who will offer you the crystal ball. If interest rates are at 6 per cent and you can lock in for five years, do it: it's not going to be of tremendous consequence if they fall to 5 per cent. You were happy with 6 per cent: live with it.

As a worst case scenario, if you are locked in at 6 per cent for five years, you could come out of the lock-in period with interest rates at 8 per cent. But as interest rates increase, so do rents, and so too do the values of properties. (Surprisingly, demand also seems to remain high. In 1988–89, for example, interest rates went as high as 17 per cent and there was a market frenzy such as I'd never seen.)

Gearing in action

Under our structure, you use the equity in your house, or put forward a cash deposit, for 10 per cent of the purchase price of a new residential investment property which—thanks to rental income and negative gearing—thereafter partly pays for itself. When the value of the property has increased by 10 per cent, you should have enough equity with the bank that loaned you the balance (assuming it is prepared to maintain a 10 per cent equity position) to acquire a second investment property. You now have two assets working for you, both increasing in value and enabling you—in a shorter period of time—to build up further equity so you can acquire your third property and so on.

Once you've acquired your second property, you're already in the charmed realm of the top individual investors because:

- 71 per cent of property investors own one property—that's 1 468 949 Australians

- 18 per cent of property investors own two properties—that's 383 505 Australians

- 5.7 per cent of property investors own three properties—that's 118 412 Australians

- 2.1 per cent own four properties—that's 43 239 Australians

- 0.88 per cent own five properties—that's 18 231 Australians

- only 0.93 per cent of Australians own six or more properties, equating to 19 198 people.

There will obviously be a limit to how many properties you can acquire over a given period of time, depending on your income, the rate of equity growth, and the amount of money your investment bank is prepared to lend you to build a portfolio. Discuss these things with a few prospective lenders. Remember, you can start small—and think big. It's not a race. Make sure you use finance to build wealth.

Let's recap

- Don't trust the banks: make sure you get a copy of your bank valuation and don't let the banks cross-collateralise your loans with your own home.

- Use a bank that understands you want to build a property portfolio using equity growth.

- Using a broker who specialises in investment loans can be valuable.

- Use your equity rather than cash.

- Borrow interest only for the first five years.

- Lock in your interest rates.

STEP 5
Aim for affordability

As I travel around Australia talking about wealth-building and residential real estate, I find that almost everybody is prepared to get excited about land appreciating (for capital growth) and buildings depreciating (for negative gearing), and about maximising income and reducing tax. There are always a few doubts, concerns and 'what if?' questions (which I address in appendix B), but there's only one really big 'yes, but...'

And that's the dreaded Real Estate Cycle.

Booms and busts. Upturns and downturns. Height of the market, depth of the recession. What happens if you buy or sell at the wrong time or at the wrong price?

Let's get some perspective about this.

Ups and downs

The idea of economic cycles is practically synonymous with real estate investment. And as usual, everyone remotely connected with the industry—and their dog—has a well-established theory about where we are in the cycle at any given time. If you talk about the history of cycles, and booms and busts, someone will always try to maintain that 'it won't happen again'—until it happens again. The bad news is that downturns do happen. The good news is that the upswings invariably follow, and that it is never 'too late' to find real opportunities for capital growth.

> **Someone will always try to maintain that 'it won't happen again'—until it happens again.**

Let me clarify something from the get-go. Property prices don't crash. They go up, they flatline, and then they go up again. That's the history. We read the term 'property crash' and 'bubble' almost every day in the newspapers, however there is no historical evidence of a property crash or a bubble bursting.

Over the past 50 years the median house price Australia-wide, which is what I'm specifically referring to, has only gone down twice: by 3 per cent in 1998 and by 4 per cent in 2011. Yes, markets that overshoot in the capital cities have minor corrections by 4 to 5 per cent, but only after a significant upturn, usually over the previous four to five years.

When I was at school, I used to work in my parents' menswear shop in country Victoria during the holidays. I'd often start work at 8.30 am, and not see a single customer until 11.00 am—and then, quite suddenly, four or five unrelated customers would walk in at the same time. You'd expect the same to happen at lunchtime, but then it would be quiet until some random point in the afternoon, when I'd be rushed off my feet all over again.

If you ever wait for trains or buses, you may recognise the same phenomenon. There is no obvious rhyme or reason to the frenzies of activity and inactivity—despite the timetable! In real estate terms, you might expect that falling interest rates would cause increased activity in the residential property market: in fact, the market was never more active than during the 1980s and 1990s when interest rates were at their highest levels.

Personally, I don't know where we are in the cycle, and I'm pretty sure that I don't need to know. I think there is a much simpler factor at work behind fluctuations in property values. And that factor is *affordability*.

Who controls the price of property?

The banks and finance companies indirectly control property prices throughout Australia. How? By controlling the amount they are prepared to lend on residential property.

And what is that decision based on? Affordability: borrowers' ability to make the necessary loan repayments, as a percentage of their income.

A typical bank lets people pay 30 to 35 per cent of their disposable income towards mortgage repayments: that's $500 per week based on the average household income of $1500 per week. This in turn determines the total amount the bank will lend over the life of the loan.

When the market is booming and banks go beyond these guidelines, weekly repayments increase to the outer limit of *everybody's* comfort zone—and that's when a crash is looming.

Table S5.1 shows mortgage repayments as a percentage of average total monthly earnings in the capital cities since 1995. In the wake of the 1989–90 recession, mortgage repayments went through the roof, and then everything came crashing down in 1991–92. The dust started to settle in 1993 with repayments reaching a manageable level. You can see that in 2003–08, during the property boom, mortgage repayments were high in comparison to the start of the decade. And what happened post 2008? The GFC, which meant mortgage repayments hit a 10-year low. The rise, fall and settling of repayments means the rise, fall and settling of property prices.

	NSW	VIC.	QLD	SA	WA
1995–96	28.77%	21.05%	23.91%	18.46%	20.96%
1996–97	31.18%	20.81%	24.27%	19.39%	19.18%
1997–98	31.51%	20.82%	20.59%	19.63%	20.22%
1999–2000	33.71%	22.94%	21.63%	18.87%	19.77%
2000–01	27.86%	24.40%	16.90%	15.96%	15.46%
2002–03	35.26%	28.37%	17.71%	18.99%	17.53%
2003–04	38.61%	30.04%	22.69%	21.52%	19.06%
2005–06	34.27%	26.85%	23.11%	22.82%	22.78%
2007–08	26.81%	24.51%	19.09%	21.29%	24.81%
2009–10	29.17%	25.09%	23.14%	22.90%	23.53%
2011–12	26.67%	25.44%	23.15%	24.74%	21.64%
2013–14	29.59%	27.65%	21.17%	22.31%	21.88%
2015–16	39.50%	32.31%	24.59%	24.18%	22.01%
2016–17	44.71%	39.86%	24.89%	25.21%	20.31%

Table S5.1: monthly mortgage repayments as a percentage of average monthly earnings

Source: ABS, REIA, RBA, CoreLogic December 2017.

Note: Mortgage payments on a 25-year loan equal 75 per cent of the median house price, at the applicable standard bank variable housing interest rate as at 30 June each year.

Making property affordable for you

I recommend building a property portfolio at the bottom end of the real estate market—that is, within a band where property is most affordable.

Monitor the value of properties *in relation to average total weekly earnings*: you can get the statistics from the Australian Bureau of Statistics in the city where you are planning to invest. Establish what you consider to be an affordable purchase price using the banks' comfort zone marker of 30 to 35 per cent as the *upper limit of what you will pay for an investment property.*

Having an upper limit of 30 to 35 per cent of average income is consistent with my suggested rental structure as well, since the price of the property will determine the rent you are able and willing to charge, and you want that to be accessible to 90 per cent of your target market.

Let's see how average property prices compare to our measure of affordability in the capital cities.

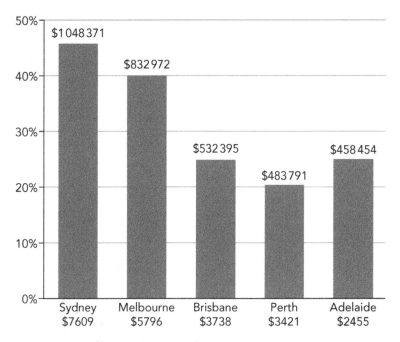

Figure S5.1: affordability based on income – average property prices showing monthly mortgage repayments as a % of average gross household income

Source: ABS 2016 Census and RP Data Median House Price Data

If you look at figure S5.1, you'll see that:

- Brisbane, Perth and Adelaide currently show good affordability: they could probably go to 35 to 40 per cent before you would start getting concerned about your ability to duplicate

- while Perth shows affordability, the concern is that it has no population growth—in fact, there has been an exodus since the end of the mining boom in 2012. So it's a market that I'm not investing in currently until I see population turnaround

- Adelaide, Brisbane and even the outskirts of Melbourne are areas I am currently investing in as there is room to move based on affordability. Melbourne in particular is a city to watch and invest in—affordability (in the outer areas) is good due to the high population growth from overseas migration.

The point is that affordability is linked to average weekly earnings and interest rates. Wages and salaries don't generally tend to fall. But you need to keep an eye on interest rates because if they rise, it can affect average property prices pretty quickly.

In the wake of the GFC, the market is unpredictable. If you study the *national* median house price over 80 years, the only time it actually fell was during a world war. And even on a state-by-state basis, over the past 30 years the median hasn't fallen off more than 10 per cent during a so-called 'crash'. Generally, house prices may flatten out for five or six years with depressed demand, but if you purchased property that was predominantly owned by occupiers, that will have been the worst of it. And it tends to affect the higher end of the market, rather than the lower end: Sydney and some parts of Melbourne may see that effect in the next few years. Lower end property still builds value well, but doesn't lose value badly when the cycle turns.

It's often purchasers paying overinflated prices for buildings that causes the mirage referred to as a 'boom'. In my experience, the fall-off in property prices mainly affects the middle to higher range house prices, where investors have paid huge premiums on buildings—inherently short-lived, replaceable products—in the mistaken perception of an under-supply. This really exposed itself during the GFC in 2008–09 where the top-end properties in all capital cities fell by 25 to 30 per cent.

> **Lower end property still builds value well, but doesn't lose it badly when the cycle turns.**

Over a 10-year period, a lot of purchasing mistakes can be recovered and redeemed in houses, but not in units, where the cushion of land content is lacking. You may be sick of me saying it by now, but (one more time): it's the land that offers capital growth; the house is just a vehicle for generating income and tax deductions in order to offset your outlays on acquiring the land.

The upside of the bottom end

Affordability cushions the effects of property cycles. It also ensures that when you decide to sell your investment property (as discussed in Step 6) you know that anybody with a job will be able to buy it. As figure S5.2 illustrates, once a property reaches $500 000 in value, less than 30 per cent of the market can afford to buy it. At about $700 000, your potential buyers make up less than 5 per cent of the 'affordable' market.

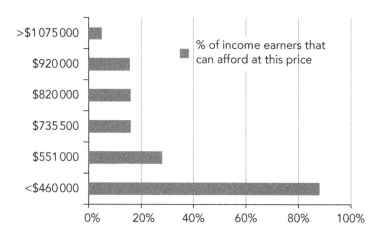

Figure S5.2: the affordable housing market

Source: ABS Cat. No. 6523: 'Household Income and Income Distribution, Australia, 2011–12'; RBA—Inflation Calculator; http://www.abs.gov.au/AUSSTATS/abs@.nsf/allprimarymainfeatures/370DA673844C5651CA257EB50011CAC2?opendocument; https://www.rba.gov.au/calculator/

Notes:
1 Based on gross household disposable income data from the ABS Cat. No. 6523: 'Household income and Income Distribution, Australia, 2011–12', adjusted with RBA Inflation Calculator to 2016 data.
2 Assuming 25 per cent deposit, P&I loan at a rate of 7 per cent and 30 per cent gross income apportioned to mortgage payments.

So, you are better off buying two properties at $500 000 each than one property at $800 000. That way, 100 per cent of the qualified market can afford to pay rent for your properties at the price you want to charge, ensuring that you optimise your income over time—especially since you have your income eggs in more than one basket, spreading the risk of vacancy or other local glitches. And 100 per cent of the qualified market can afford to buy your properties whenever you wish to liquidate your assets.

MAKE IT AFFORDABLE

One of my good clients is a top surgeon who is in the highest income bracket, earning in excess of $1 million per year. He could obviously afford to buy a $5 to $10 million property. After reading *7 Steps to Wealth* and coming along to my seminars and meeting me, we devised a strategy for him to build a portfolio and a land bank that will give him income in retirement.

Over the past 10 years he's created a portfolio of 17 properties in four states to minimise his land tax. All the properties are cash flow positive, but they also give him a much-needed tax deduction as a result of depreciation. The beauty of his portfolio is that he has a land bank of 9700 m² and the majority of the properties are adjoining, which gives him several parcels of land in excess of 1000 m². When he's ready to retire in five to 10 years I'd expect he'll have 15 000 m² of land; and with density and zoning conditions improving, instead of that land bank supplying 20 tenants, it could supply up to 50 tenants with granny flats, auxiliary dwellings, student accommodation and so on.

This case study demonstrates again that no matter what your income, affordability is a key factor in developing an investment property portfolio that suits you and your tenants.

Let's recap

- There's no historical evidence of a property crash.

- Market cycles fluctuate: they go up; they're flat for maybe seven or eight years; and then they go up again.

- Banks and finance companies indirectly control property prices throughout Australia by controlling the amount they are prepared to lend on residential property. Affordability calculators used by the banks are one measure of room for growth.

- Affordability is linked to average weekly earnings and interest rates.

In Step 6 we'll look at if, when and how to sell your investment properties to maximise capital growth and make time work for you.

Make time work for you

Some people trade in the property market—constantly buying and selling—quite successfully.

Actually, when I say 'some' people, I mean perhaps 0.01 per cent of investors.

Buying and selling property is *expensive*: 12 to 16 per cent of the initial purchase price can be thrown away in stamp duty, fees, charges, commission on resale and so on. This is often the forgotten factor when people buy 'fixer uppers'. They add value through renovation and onsell at a higher price, but rarely at a price high enough to offset the costs of renovation *and* the costs of buying and selling!

As you may have noticed, the wealth-building concept is a longer term acquisition plan. It's based on long-term factors (such as the historical capital growth of residential house-and-land packages, and building equity) and offers long-term benefits.

Building wealth using our structure means you don't get rich quickly; you get rich slowly. The key is to buy, and keep buying, and to *hold*. In other words, you have to adopt the following formula:

Assets + Time = Wealth

Time works—when you do!

I could have called this step 'Time for discipline'. A lot of people get excited by the growth history of property and the prospect of building serious wealth—but they often lack the discipline, patience and commitment to see it through.

Ironically, this is especially true of some of the high-powered executive types who come to our seminars. They're happy to agree with all the principles, but confess that building wealth, the way I portray it, simply isn't as exciting as going out, doing a deal and making hundreds of thousands of dollars in one 'hit'.

Fair enough. I've got to admit that our wealth-building structure is not all that exciting. It's not a thrill-a-minute gamble. It asks you to wait and 'watch the grass grow'. But there's also a reasonable expectation that beneath that grass—in the land—lie dollars and capital appreciation!

Let me tell you the biggest mistake you can ever make in real estate: selling. Selling land is always a mistake because it will always appreciate. My mentors taught me that and I want to teach you that. Even if I think about the example I gave earlier where I sold my land in Byron Bay for a massive profit, I still absolutely know one day I will look back and say, 'What was I thinking?' (Actually, what I was thinking was to use the proceeds to buy more work horses and acquire more land.)

Let's go back to our muscle-building analogy in chapter 3. Muscle only grows when it is rested. When muscle-builders become overenthusiastic, or

> **Our wealth-building structure is not all that exciting.**

downright impatient, and do not rest sufficiently after carrying out an exercise, they end up breaking down from stress. Unfortunately, this can occur in financial situations, too, so banks, accountants and advisors are the first ones to point out if your business has grown too quickly or too soon, and to advise you to put the brakes on.

Making time work for you is really about establishing the discipline and commitment to acquire six properties over a 10-year period, and building on the history of the past 90 years to plan for 8 per cent per annum capital growth.

Let's look again at the basic financial goal for duplication that we introduced in chapter 3, before all our steps to wealth were in place.

Have a look at figure S6.1 and S6.2 (overleaf) to see where you could end up if you start today by purchasing the kind of property we've talked about in Steps 1 to 5 priced at $500 000.

Buy 3 homes over 10 years at 8% capital growth
Asset growth
Optional sale
Year 1
Year 2
Year 3
Year 4
Year 5
Year 6
Year 7
Year 8
Year 9
Year 10
Year 11
Year 12
At year 12 net assets $1.92 million | Positive income $61134 p.a.

Figure S6.1: financial goals—three homes over 10 years

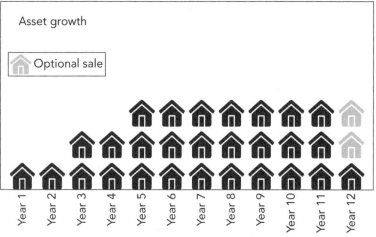

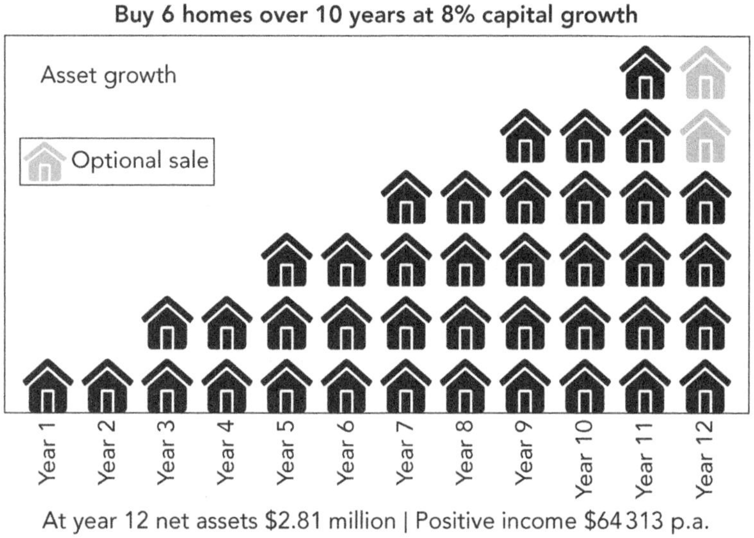

Buy 6 homes over 10 years at 8% capital growth
Asset growth
Optional sale
Year 1
Year 2
Year 3
Year 4
Year 5
Year 6
Year 7
Year 8
Year 9
Year 10
Year 11
Year 12
At year 12 net assets $2.81 million | Positive income $64313 p.a.

Figure S6.2: financial goals—six homes over 10 years

Okay. Are you sitting down?

If you acquire three properties over five years:

- you will have paid $1 853 444 for your portfolio *and*
- you will have a debt of $1 853 444 (if you don't pay off any of your principal).

If you acquire six properties over a 10-year period:

- you will have paid $4 741 809 for your portfolio and
- you will have a debt of $4 741 809 (if you don't pay off any of the principal).

Just let that sink in for a moment. It may sound scary. But remember: you will also have sufficient *income* to service that entire debt *and* many of your other outlays (based on interest rates of 7 per cent).

And here are some more reassuring—perhaps even exciting—numbers.

- In year 10, a three-property portfolio would be worth around $3 238 387 and growing by nearly $250 000 per annum. And in year 12, you'd have net assets of around $1 923 811, still growing at that stage by over $250 000 per annum.

- In year 10, a six-property portfolio would be worth around $6 476 775 and growing by nearly $500 000 per annum. And in year 12, you'd have net assets of around $2 812 701, and growing by more than $500 000 per annum.

If that doesn't make you feel any happier, let's put those debt numbers into perspective.

- If you'd started building a six-property portfolio around 1965, today *the land value alone* would be *more than $4.5 million*. And even if you'd borrowed

100 per cent and never paid a cent of principal, you would have debt of less than $140 000.

- If you'd started building a six-property portfolio around 1975, the land value alone would also be *$4.5 million* today, and—without having repaid any of the principal—your debt would be around $350 000.

- If you'd started building a six-property portfolio in 1985, you'd have a land value of *more than $4 million* today, with a debt—again, without having repaid any of the principal—of *$1 million*.

You'd also have rental *income* from the six properties, which would easily service a P&I loan *and* give you some income, *and* you'd have capital growth of more than $400 000 a year, which will continue to *compound*.

The debts that you might have been carrying from the 1960s, 1970s or 1980s wouldn't seem so scary when you think of where you're at now. This may be a helpful perspective for starting your wealth-building.

Although, with three properties, $1 853 444 (in 10 years) may seem to be a lot of debt to carry:

- it is being reliably serviced without drawing too heavily on your personal cash flow or other resources

- your equity is growing by $250 000.

People often challenge me with the assertion that since inflation is low, property won't grow at the same rate. Indeed, I read all sorts of 'expert' opinions preaching this as some new financial gospel. Where do they get it from? If you stayed awake to the property markets around Australia, for example, during the period 1997–2000, you'd be aware that property tends to rebound to make up for limited capital growth in slower years. We need to look coolly at the effects of inflation. During the 1960s, we had an average inflation rate of approximately

2.5 per cent—and property prices in some capital cities grew at a massive 13 per cent per annum.

My personal opinion is that inflation really just props up building costs, and therefore *units*, which have a high building content. And, throughout the 1960s, 1970s and 1980s, the growth in *house* values, as a percentage, outperformed units and townhouses.

How do you make time work for you?

From a long-term perspective, there need be no barriers to wealth-building. It merely requires a disciplined commitment in two areas:

1. *keep buying* over the 10-year period (unless the principle of affordability has been made impossible by a greedy phase of the market in a particular area)

2. *take one step at a time.*

We'll look at each of these commitments in turn.

Keep buying

With an average property growth of 8 per cent over any 10-year period, you will have six opportunities to use your increased equity to acquire further property. You might be 'sitting out' of the market for perhaps three years out of the 10.

The time to sit out of the market is when the factors in property pricing (indirectly controlled, as we noted, by the lending institutions) are out of step with average income, and therefore beyond the level of general affordability in a particular area.

Remember the table of mortgage repayments as a percentage of average weekly earnings in Step 5 (table S5.1)?

Things went crazy in 1989 and 1990 in Sydney and Melbourne, as repayments reached between 60 and 78 per cent of average earnings.

House prices came off slightly in 1991 before settling down in 1992 and 1993. If we were building a portfolio at this time, monitoring the market according to our principle of affordability, we would have sat out of the market in Sydney and Melbourne from 1988 right through to 1991. We could have come back in 1992, perhaps even picking up prime opportunities because of the desperation of a panicked market, in which the banks sell up less careful investors. This is called *counter-cyclical buying*. The moral is: don't be a herd investor. Don't buy when everybody else does—that is, when property begins to rise. Buy when everyone else is selling, and sell when everyone else is buying. Better yet: never sell!

Sydney and Melbourne seem particularly vulnerable to boom-time problems, perhaps because of the density and size of their populations and the confidence that the banks derive from having their head offices located in those cities, where they deal with major corporate players. Notice that in Brisbane, Adelaide and Perth there was nowhere near the same frenzy of mortgage repayments being out of kilter with affordability.

You might have chosen to sit out of the market in Brisbane during 1989–90—but even if you bought during those times, your capital appreciation still would have shown some growth in 1991–93.

In any case, if you use your affordability principles, you can judge when to wait and when to buy again without over-reaching yourself or slowing your capital growth. And in order to accelerate and maintain your portfolio development, remember: *you do need to keep buying.*

As we noted in Step 4, around 2 per cent of all individual investors acquire more than four properties. With a bit of discipline and commitment to keep buying, you will put yourself among the very top wealth-builders.

One step at a time

Acquiring six properties over a 10- to 12-year period—and holding onto them as a retirement plan—*works*.

Of course, you could accelerate or slow down this process to suit your own capacity and confidence.

The important point is to take it one step at a time.

> **Acquiring six properties over a 10-year period—and holding onto them as a retirement plan—*works*.**

Don't be mesmerised at this stage by the thought of owing $3 million, or having to manage six properties. Like climbing a mountain, it may look a long way from the bottom to the top, but you get there one step at a time…and one property at a time. Give yourself a year or two to settle in, to work out some of the kinks and to establish your structure firmly so that there really is no drain on your resources. Let your confidence build with each successful step. And then, when the fresh equity is there, think about purchasing again.

Some people say to me that they just *can't* come to grips with the idea of that amount of debt, or owning six properties: they think because they can't see themselves, as they are today, going from *here* to *there* all of a sudden, that it's just not for

> **Like climbing a mountain, it may look a long way from the bottom to the top, but you get there one step at a time…**

them. That's like letting the mountain conquer you before you have even taken a step. The thing to remember is that:

- you don't have to do it all at once—just one step at a time

- you don't have to do the whole journey with the resources or the perspective that you start with: the journey itself equips you as you go forward.

Knowing your options

'Making time work for you' means trusting that all your resources (equity, knowledge, experience, perspective) will grow and mature as the journey proceeds. You now have enough knowledge to get started. And, with this structure, *you are in control*. At each step—as at the 'end' of the journey—there are *options* depending on what you want to achieve and what the market is doing.

The three most attractive options are:

1. convert your loan to P&I after 5 years
2. sell, and repay your debt
3. redevelop with higher density zoning.

Let's now look at each of these in turn.

1 Convert your loan to P&I after 5 years

I personally like the strategy of converting the investment loan on a property to principal and interest (P&I) after you have owned that property for five years. Rental income growth of between 3 per cent and 4 per cent per annum should allow you to convert your interest-only loan to P&I in year 6 or 7—and *still* maintain a minimal cash outlay.

Over time, the tenant will then be paying off your mortgage.

You should be aware that the principal is not tax deductible, so you may, following conversion of the loan, have to pay tax. You should also be aware that in the first five years of a 20-year P&I

loan, you only pay off between 12 per cent and 15 per cent of the total principal: it is in the last five years that you really see the compound effect of your principal repayments. However, this is a step in the right direction, and can give you some peace of mind if you're looking to pay off the principal on multiple properties and hold onto them (as they keep generating income) as a retirement plan and/or to pass onto your kids.

2 Sell, and repay your debt

Selling one or more of your properties is, of course, an option for reducing some or all of the debt on the rest of your portfolio. You need to think about:

- what to sell
- when to sell.

Selling is particularly attractive in a boom time when the market may be more optimistic than realistic.

The best time to sell is when everyone else is buying. And that includes that typical two-year peak in the 'cycle' when affordability parameters seem to have gone out the window! You could see the value of your portfolio increase by 25 to 30 per cent *above* its 'true' value for a two-year period (before coming down). Some investors—and a lot of speculators—try to take advantage of this cyclical movement that we've learned to identify.

So what happens if you take advantage of the cyclical peak?

Well, if you sold your *last* two properties (acquired in years 8 and 10, with the cycle working in your favour), in year 12 at the peak of the market, instead of an average 30 per cent increase, you might have a 50 per cent increase on your purchase price. So, if the properties cost you $1.3 million and are now worth $1.6 million, you may have an opportunity to sell them for $1.9 million: a profit of $600 000 instead of $300 000.

Capital gains tax for individuals

When you sell (or otherwise dispose of) an asset acquired after 19 September 1985, you are liable for capital gains tax (CGT) on any increased value, or profit. In terms of property, your *home* is exempt—however, investment property, unfortunately, isn't. Highly simplified, the amount of taxable capital gain is calculated as the sale price (consideration) *minus* the acquisition cost of the property, adjusted by the depreciation claimed on it, and reduced by 50 per cent where the property has been held for a period of 12 months or more.

In example 1, CGT is worked out on the $290 000 profit, discounted by 50 per cent. So if you held those last two properties for two years and three years respectively, the calculation would work as follows.

EXAMPLE 1: CALCULATING CGT ON 2 PROPERTIES HELD FOR 2 AND 3 YEARS RESPECTIVELY

	Property 5 (Year 9)	Property 6 (Year 10)	Total (Year 12)
Purchase price	$999 000	$1 079 000	$2 078 000
Building allowance	$14 000	$11 000	$25 000
Sale price	$1 259 000	$1 259 000	$2 518 000
Book profit	$260 000	$180 000	$440 000
Less			
Capital gain	$247 000	$191 000	$465 000
50% discount	$137 000	$95 000	$232 500
Equals			
Taxable profit (gain)	$137 000	$95 000	$232 500

You would have to pay CGT on a total of $144 000 (after 12 years of investment). This would amount to $67 680 based on the *highest* marginal rate of income tax.

Four points to note:

1. The calculation applies to all property purchased by individuals after 21 September 1999 (when the CGT rules changed) that is held for 12 months prior to sale. If a property is held for less than 12 months, you must pay tax on the total book profit.

2. Where a property was purchased prior to 21 September 1999, you have the option of calculating the amount of your taxable gain using the above discount method or you may choose to calculate the taxable gain as the sale price (consideration received) *minus* the acquisition cost of the property, indexed for inflation to 30 September 1999. (Don't panic. Most people don't do their own CGT calculations: they keep their basic purchase/expenditure/sale records and hand them over to a competent accountant, which I highly recommend doing.)

3. If you've sold during a boom, the property may well have been inflated above its true value by almost the total amount of tax you have to pay! So waiting for the boom glitch in the cycle, and taking that opportunity to sell, is a way of minimising the impact of CGT.

4. There's a lot of talk around tax changes in relation to property as more people retire, making pension payments a strain on the government. The effect on CGT may be that instead of having a 50 per cent threshold, after an election the threshold may be reduced to 25 per cent.

Goods and services tax (GST)

Since the introduction of a goods and services tax (GST) on 1 July 2000, it is necessary to consider its impact on the sale of property. Before a sale can be subject to GST, however, you must be registered for the GST. You only need to become registered when your annual turnover exceeds $75 000 *excluding* rental income, salary and wages.

The short version of the story is that unless you are in the business of buying and selling newly constructed properties on a regular basis (i.e. buying or selling more than one new property every 12 months) you should not need to register for the GST. If you don't need to register, you don't need to include the GST in the price for which you sell the property. (This position will be different if you are conducting a business in your name. Again this should be clarified with a competent accountant.)

Tax is simply a factor of doing business.

Tax is simply a factor of doing business. It's one of the reasons why you might consider *not* selling, but *holding* your properties as they keep generating income over time. If you are selling on a regular basis (which is not recommended) then GST may be a factor.

3 Redevelop with higher density zoning

As we have noted, the population in Australia's major cities is steadily growing.

The solution developed by town planners over the past few years is *urban infill*—that is, the redevelopment of 600 m² and 700 m² blocks to accommodate two, three or four dwellings instead of one. This may be an option for you in 20 to

30 years' time, if you're still holding a portfolio (as I recommend). Remember, it's the *land* that's of value.

You won't be able to take advantage of higher density building if you own a townhouse, or if you share land with another landlord in a group title, but owning a house does give you this flexibility. In Melbourne, Sydney and Brisbane, they have already allowed dual occupancy, and it won't be long (10 to 20 years) before higher density zoning will again be allowed on these smaller lots. This may effectively give you the opportunity, with your equity, to build three to four income-generating properties on your allotment. I'd still encourage you not to sell them, but to keep the land for further growth.

This has been the secret of a lot of car yards, which bought fringe CBD sites on main roads 10 to 20 years ago, and now find those sites are commanding a premium and being re-developed as fast-food restaurants, shopping centres and so on. Even if their businesses have only broken even, these car dealers are very wealthy individuals today because they owned and held onto the land.

The global financial crisis (GFC)

It is interesting to look back at housing affordability in Australia. The residential markets on the east coast had a tremendous run in price growth in 1997, 1998 and 2003. My clients and I were principally buying in Brisbane and to a lesser extent in Melbourne during those times.

Back in 2003, the markets on the east coast peaked, as did affordability. However, this created an opportunity to buy on the west coast, in Perth. While property on the east coast was selling for mid $300 000 in 2004–05, we were buying property in Perth in the $200 000 range in 2003–05. The market in Perth significantly increased in value. By 2006, everything we had purchased in 2003–05 increased to around $500 000. As we moved back to the east coast in 2007–09, we were able to continue buying in and around Brisbane and Melbourne in the $300 000 market in good locations.

Properties around the $300 000 mark looked very affordable even during the GFC, which really hit Australia around 2009 to 2013.

In 2009 we found Melbourne and Sydney appealing again and bought many thousands of properties.

We bought house-and-land packages, with land at around $500 per square metre and houses for $1250 per square metre in the inner west and north of Melbourne (with total packages of around $380 000). The land alone today is worth upwards of $750 to $800 per square metre.

In 2011, we started looking at Sydney after doing our numbers: from 2003 to 2011 the median house price in Sydney had barely gone up 10 per cent. More importantly, the population growth in Sydney between 2001 and 2011 was $500 000, and we knew there were only approximately 50 000 new blocks of land being built during the same period in greater Sydney due to a dispute the government was having with councils and developers. In other words, it was almost a perfect storm having a GFC and no supply, which created a lot of pent-up demand—and a Sydney boom!

We acquired 416 house-and-land packages in Sydney in 2011–14. The average allotment size was 426 square metres at an average price of $598 per square metre. Today, the average land value of our allotments is $1313 per square metre, which reflects a growth of 120 per cent. In the same period the Sydney median house price increased by 92 per cent. More to the point, when we bought our properties the rental returns were 5.8 per cent and all of our clients were cash flow positive and were therefore able to use their cash flow and growth to duplicate again.

Interestingly, when we announced to all our clients around Australia that we were going into the Sydney market at the end of 2011, it was our Sydney clients who were reluctant to buy. Our Brisbane, Melbourne and Perth clients were buying the Sydney properties. It's the old saying, 'you don't see the forest for the trees'. Some of my clients were saying to me, 'John, Sydney is a basket case. It will never recover. You shouldn't be buying here'... The rest is history.

The confidence factor

In order to build wealth successfully—and not stressfully—you need to be confident. Having confidence in something new can be difficult because if you look too far ahead, you can scare yourself by 'seeing' all kinds of mirages of things that might go wrong, and that you may well not know how to deal with (yet). The thing about mirages is, when you actually get there, they tend to disappear.

In appendix B, I answer some of the 'What if?' and 'What about?' questions that you might still have so that you will be more informed, and hopefully this will help you feel more confident. I get those questions all the time. And it's great—it's vital—that they get asked because knowledge builds confidence. When you're about to start a journey, it's natural to look for potholes in the road. As I said right at the start, sceptics make the best wealth-builders. But the fact is, no-one's got a crystal ball. There's no such thing as having 'all the answers' (or even 'all the questions') ahead of time. Sooner or later, you've got to choose to take a first step—and that's when the real answers start coming.

You've just read up on data, pros and cons, principles and options, and suggestions. I'm glad if you feel better informed now than when you started this book. But I'd also like you to keep sight of our starting point: the sense of a journey, and the new possibilities that open up as you dare to think about creating wealth for yourself and others.

So in Step 7, let's look, one more time, at where we're headed.

Let's recap

- The benefits of letting time work for you are enormous: have another look at figures S6.1 and S6.2 to see what you can achieve in 12 years.

- Building wealth using our structure means you don't get rich quickly; you get rich slowly. The key is to buy, keep buying and hold.

- You need discipline, patience and commitment to see it through.

- Take one step at a time.

- At each step of the investment journey there are options depending on what you want to achieve and what the market is doing. The options include converting your loan to P&I after 5 years; selling, and repaying your debt; or redeveloping with higher density zoning.

- Confidence is a major part of successful—not stressful—wealth-building.

- Let me give you some time-honoured and proven advice: the biggest mistake you'll ever make in real estate is selling land.

Be all you can be

Early on in this book, I hoped to plant a seed in your mind that, as you begin to build wealth, you may find yourself getting back more than you expected—more than just financial rewards. I shared with you my own belief that everything has a purpose—and that, through building wealth, I began to discover mine. I'd always felt I had potential—but for what? I started out with the goal of being wealthy, and it was as I reached that goal that I found the goal posts had moved forever.

How do you feel about the idea of being wealthy? Powerful? Excited? Quietly secure—is it just a way to meet your day-to-day needs and those of your family? Or perhaps a little bit guilty or embarrassed? (Some people do.) What possibilities are you allowing yourself to look forward to? And are they really the best you can expect *for* yourself—and *of* yourself?

One of the qualities shared by wealthy people is that they are pro-active: they see opportunities and make things happen. You may have glimpsed an opportunity as you read this book. You may even go out and make it happen. And being pro-active tends to make you *more* pro-active because when you're out there, you begin to notice things that you may not have noticed before, and to have the confidence to do something about them. This kind of mental preparedness may be part of your potential: imagine how useful it could be in all sorts of areas of your life.

Wealth: the big picture

Approximately 0.0001 per cent of the world's population controls 99 per cent of the world's wealth.

Apparently, a computer model has demonstrated that if all that wealth was distributed equally among every living person, within about 15 years it would have filtered back to the 0.0001 per cent. Whether this is true or not, isn't it an amazing concept? What it means to me is that those few of us who are fortunate and knowledgeable enough to create, control and enjoy wealth have a responsibility towards those who aren't and don't. We are not just wealthy individuals: we are custodians of the world's wealth in our society.

> **We are not just wealthy individuals: we are custodians of the world's wealth in our society.**

And that means if you're in the wealth-building business, you have a purpose and a responsibility *wider* than meeting your own needs and the needs of your family.

Some people talk as if 'you can't take it with you' is a negative thing, and a reason not to bother creating wealth at all. Personally, I find it an energising and empowering idea. I can't take my wealth with me: therefore, I'll both *enjoy it*—and *pass it on*. While I'm alive, I'm 'minding' a portion of the world's wealth, and I can 'pass it on' in all sorts of ways: by improving living conditions and opportunities for others now, and by self-sustaining capital and wealth-preserving knowledge for the future.

There comes a time in your wealth-building journey when you realise that you have 'enough' wealth to be able to retire. It became clear to me in 1990 that I was getting close: by

> **All that man is, is infinite. All that man has, is finite.**

1991, I could have retired with an annual income of $300000 for the rest of my life. It was what I'd always thought I wanted, but when I got there, retiring on my wealth seemed like a huge cop-out. I still needed a challenge and a purpose. At the same time, I couldn't see making *more* (and more) money, for the sake of it, as very fulfilling or purposeful. And that's when the 'custodian' perspective kicked in for me.

Toogoolawa

I decided to establish my own charitable foundation for homeless youth, whose plight had concerned me for some time. As 'luck' (or whatever) would have it, I met psychologists Dr Ron and Suwanti Farmer, and together we established the Toogoolawa Children's Home. We started out in Sydney, providing full-time residential care to youth at risk (generally wards of the state) whose family life had psychologically damaged them.

'Toogoolawa': a place in the heart

'Toogoolawa' is an aboriginal word meaning 'a place in the heart': our belief is that, no matter what physical abuse children have suffered, there is a place within themselves where they can find healing, strength and meaning.

Toogoolawa has fostered more than 500 young people with tremendous success. Some boys as young as 11 and 12 had lived in up to 18 other foster homes before coming to Toogoolawa. Many of them stay with us until they are 15 or 16 years old and ready to live independently. As coincidence would have it, as I was completing the final edit of this edition I received an email from one of our first residents. He is now 40 years old and living in the United States, and he emailed me to tell me he had just been promoted to Vice President of Merrill Lynch Bank and wanted to share the good news with me. I am so proud of him.

In 1993, we moved the home to Brisbane and since then we have focused on what we found was the real missing link: education. We now operate as Toogoolawa Schools Limited.

The Toogoolawa Schools

The first school was established in 1998 on the Pimpama Rivers Estate I developed at Ormeau in south-east Queensland. It offers education and opportunity to kids who have either been expelled or excluded from mainstream schools. When we began to research the need, we were alarmed to find that every year there were up to 300 children aged under 15 in the Brisbane area alone who had been expelled from the public school system and weren't attending school.

I don't blame the public school system: these kids are, quite often, 'difficult' and disruptive in a 'normal' classroom environment due to the stress and trauma they have experienced at home. Every study on education tells us that for kids to learn, they need to be in a happy environment, and that's our challenge at Toogoolawa. We have a saying that they are either mad, bad or sad. But, to be honest, they are simply highly stressed and traumatised youth who have had an upbringing that is unimaginable for many people. Nevertheless, they have a right to — and we have a responsibility to offer them — some type of education. (This is another area where 'expert' opinions and statistics are rampant. I'm not going to labour the point, but it may interest you to learn that, of the prison population in Australia, 95 per cent are from broken families and more than 60 per cent are illiterate. Perhaps, if we start with change in these areas, as a community we can begin to turn around the social decay that we are all so aware of and so frequently daunted by. As with wealth-building, start small and think big. Radical change happens one step at a time.)

The Toogoolawa Schools offer a basic education and a simple, positive philosophy to live by: that service, truthfulness and consideration for others leads

> **Radical change happens one step at a time.**

to a happy, fulfilled and effective life. The students are taught not only to read, write and spell, but to speak, listen and calculate—as well as to strive to discern right from wrong, and to see the value in following the former.

The Toogoolawa School at Ormeau also operates as a mobile unit, utilising the ideal learning environment of the outdoors. By combining fun and physical activity with experiential learning techniques, students begin to see learning as immediate and relevant, and develop a sense of responsibility for their choices and actions.

The five universal human values of love, truth, peace, right-conduct and non-violence are integrated into all aspects of the school curriculum. The teachers endeavour to become role models for these values, and convey to the students that these qualities already lie within each one of them, like a diamond hidden inside a mountain.

As we teach the kids, we recognise that there can be many difficult things going on in their lives—as there are in the wider world—and we remind them there is always a place in their heart where they can find safety, security and solace.

Regular sharing sessions help to develop communication skills. A sense of community is important too: students regularly visit a nursing home for the elderly, and assist at a work facility (SWARA) for the developmentally disabled as part of our commitment to community service. We strive for a balance between *support* (with an emphasis on social interaction and exploration of spirituality and ecology) and *challenge*, in order to empower and inspire our students to acknowledge and achieve their potential.

A small difference makes a big difference

At Toogoolawa, we see kids who don't trust anyone because of the hurt they've sustained in the supposed 'sanctuary' of their own homes. Their distress bursts out in anger and aggression. And so it begins: they go from home to home and from school to school, setting themselves up for rejection after rejection, the only pattern they've ever known.

But at Toogoolawa, we've seen the vicious circle broken. Some of the kids spend the rest of their adolescence with us, which means we can begin to help them work through some of their problems. We can give them time to discover that what has happened to them isn't the best they can expect from other people. And that there is some goodness in the world—and within themselves.

We have a ratio of social workers to students higher than any other school in Australia and we focus on getting the kids to feel good about themselves and teaching them what they need for a healthy future.

Let me tell you how I've started my week for the past 20 years. On Monday morning I arrive at the school between 8.45 am and 9 am for 'quiet time'. The teachers, social workers and I sit in a large circle with all the students. Some days there are more than 100 people in the room. Gerry, our headmaster at Pimpama, holds up a feather and wishes everybody a good morning. Then he passes the feather to the next person in the circle and they wish the whole room a good morning. This is repeated until everybody in the room has wished the others a good morning. When that's done, one of the students kneels down and lights a candle, which is our ritual, and as he lights the candle he says, 'When we light these flames, we light the flames of love, truth, peace, right-conduct and non-violence within us all' and then in unison we say our sacred words: 'We start the day with love; we fill the day with love; we end the day with love. This is the way we live'.

I promise you, when 100 people in a room do that, something changes in the cells of your body and I've seen the changes in the new kids at school from their first day to after having done this for three months. It's amazing.

Then Gerry, I or one of the teachers starts a meditation. We focus on the breath, watching it go in and out, to teach the boys that if we slow our breath down, we slow our brains down. We watch the breath for five to 10 minutes and then we use a mantra, where we say a word such as 'toogoolawa' or 'maranatha' (from Corinthians 16:22; meaning 'Come, Lord') as we breathe in and out. The meditation can go for 15 to 20 minutes.

After this, we tell a story using the thought for the week. If it's my turn to tell the story I might talk about Gandhi as a boy and all the fears and afflictions he suffered and how he learned to cope and not only overcome them but become a world leader living the five human values we teach. We then talk to the boys about this and how they can use it in their lives, so that no matter what trauma they're going through, they always have a place in their heart that they can go to.

So that's how I start my week — and how we start a week at Toogoolawa School. It makes me feel blessed and it's a privilege.

At Toogoolawa we have had to reinvent education in a lot of ways, and I am proud to say that the state and federal governments have acknowledged this by giving us a $3 million building grant in recognition of our school being leading edge. This has enabled us to build a new classroom for manual arts and hospitality, and outdoor recreation and quiet-time areas for the boys, which will symbolise our growth and success for many years to come.

Like wealth-building, it's a long-term program: no quick fixes. When kids first come to us, they are — understandably — pretty angry. Three years later, you can see the anger being channelled into something more positive and supportive for them. They have begun to develop some self-esteem, and to feel good about themselves, perhaps for the first time in their lives.

Sowing the seed

As you can probably tell, I'm pretty committed to—and excited by—my work with the Toogoolawa project. Over the past 20 years, I have committed more than $10 million in total to this project. And the fact is, it's been enriching: perhaps the most fulfilling thing I've done in my life.

I started out only providing the money to run the program and assist with the administration (we have a great team of psychologists and social workers who work hands-on with the kids and are a constant inspiration to me and to others who come to see the Toogoolawa effect in action). But I was soon challenged to give something more of myself, running outdoor education and effective communication classes, allowing me to share my passion for hiking with the kids.

It's making a small difference that makes a big difference.

We all share the responsibility to maintain humanity, justice and opportunity in our society. My hope is that other businesses could take responsibility—and find purpose—in funding similar programs. They have the resources and administrative capabilities that welfare agencies often lack.

I am also very proud to say that the teaching techniques used in Toogoolawa are being studied and often adopted in other schools. We have even had several teachers from schools in other countries visit us to see what we do. In fact, Dr Ron and

Suwanti Farmer have travelled to eight different countries, on invitation from schools there, to lecture on Toogoolawa.

The Farmers also have a teacher training program that they now run two to three times per year for 20 to 50 teachers at a time looking for skills on how to engage disengaged youth. If you are a teacher and want to learn more you can find out more on the Toogoolawa website.

So, if, like me, you feel that being all you can be goes further than achieving wealth for yourself and your family, let me encourage you: it needn't be too far away. Once you have a portfolio of four or five homes, you could use the equity to purchase an older home, which you could dedicate to people in need.

> **If you feel that being all you can be goes further than achieving wealth for yourself and your family, let me encourage you: it needn't be too far away.**

Why an older home? Well, it depends what you are going to use it for, but we had one great kid at Toogoolawa who used to have a monthly fit of rage and frustration—and put his fist through the wall. (He was with us for three years, and by the end, those rages were down to one every six months. He was responsible for repairing and repainting the wall himself—and he got quite good at it. It was amazing to see the pride he took in patching and painting the plaster, and decorating his room so that the damage—like the anger—didn't have to be a daily part of his life.)

The acquisition can be structured so that the interest can be claimed as a negatively geared tax deduction, and you could still get the benefit of capital growth, despite the building's age.

Alternatively, if you'd just like to know more about the Toogoolawa Schools and others like them, you may want to read my book *We Can Be Heroes*: the extraordinary stories of some 'ordinary' Australians who make a real difference in the world one step at a time. Or just call us and ask about what we do: we'd love to hear from you. You'll find contact details at the back of this book.

The small difference that makes a big difference...

I'd like to tell you a story told to me by Dr Ron Farmer.

An old man went down to the beach in the morning, where the surf roared onto the still cool sand at the lowest part of the tide. The beach was covered with starfish stranded by the tide as far as the eye could see. The old man bent down and began picking up the starfish and throwing them, one by one, back into the water.

A young runner in a grey tracksuit passed and stopped. He turned around and said, 'What are you doing? Can't you see that you're wasting your time? There are hundreds of starfish here. Throwing a few back won't make a bit of difference'.

The old man bent over and picked up another rough shape in his rough hand and threw the starfish out into the water with a quiet splash. Then he said, 'It made a difference to that one'.

Finding a wider, deeper purpose for your wealth-building can enrich you on many levels. It can provide the fire and commitment you need to keep going—to start small and think big: it can positively contribute to your success in building wealth. More importantly, perhaps, it can stretch what you may have seen as the limits of your potential, and what it means to be all you can be.

Jason McCartney's story

Recently, the human importance of what we do at Custodian was summarised so well by Jason McCartney, Australian hero, AFL player and long-term client of mine, when he spoke at our annual Kick Start event. He personally, and generously, related how being a Custodian client helped both him and his wife in their time of dire need.

HOW CUSTODIAN HELPED ME

I looked at a few property groups before I became part of the Custodian group in 1998. And, it's been a fantastic journey. At one stage my wife and I had six properties. Through the miracle of compound growth that John speaks about so often, we chose to capitalise on and sell three of those properties in order to fund our family home in Melbourne. Only recently have we recommitted to our wealth-building journey by purchasing another property.

My background is AFL. I played with Collingwood, Adelaide and the North Melbourne Kangaroos. In 2002, I unfortunately found myself caught up in the Bali terrorist attacks in Paddy's Bar. I was only 5 metres away from where the first of the explosions went off, set there by a suicide bomber. I sustained burns to 50 per cent of my body, my eardrums were perforated and I sustained numerous shrapnel wounds.

When I go back to that time in hospital in 2002 in my mind, I remember sitting there—lying there, as I couldn't do much else—knowing Nerissa was really concerned with trying to think about all the things she had to take care of at home. I remember one thing she asked: 'What about the investment properties? What do I need to do about them, Jason?'

'You don't have to do anything,' I said with some confidence. 'Custodian is a well-structured program. They're well set up and they'll take care of themselves.' And they did.

That's what I've found with Custodian. Once you get set up and get started, it will take care of itself. And what I said to my wife then is still true: 'It'll be okay … it'll be fine'. And it has been.

Obviously it was a very difficult period for my family, and me, as I found myself in a hospital, fighting for life. But, I had amazing support. I think that's what's really important with whatever you do. That ability to set goals and challenge yourself—but you need outstanding people around you and I certainly had that and more.

It was a struggle. But I had tremendous support and with that, and determination, in three and a half weeks—much to the surprise of my surgeons and the people at the Alfred Hospital—I was released. A rehabilitation program came next with the ultimate goal of me getting back to playing AFL football again. But before that I had a more immediate goal to achieve.

The Bali bombings happened in October and my wedding to Nerissa had been planned for 14 December of that same year. So, that was my first, real short-term goal. To really focus and work and drive towards marrying my girl. I was not given all that much hope, but we got there. And there is no doubt in my mind that the determination to make that ceremony helped me to kick start the journey into getting back and playing AFL football. One thing supported the next … and the next …

So, the goal to continue my career followed. However, throughout the process I realised I knew little about burn injuries and soon I knew I had a long, long road ahead. It would take two to three years to fully recover.

My next goal was to get back and play, yes, but the ultimate was to play one game only. I was able to achieve that milestone on the 6th June during the 2003 season, where I returned to play for the Kangaroos against Richmond. What an amazing night that was. The main objective was achieved as we won that game, most importantly! From a personal point of view, I was thankful I could play my part by kicking a goal and helping to set up the last one that ultimately got us across the line, but when you are involved in a team, it's about team success. And the team did it.

From there it's been about the next phase of my life: retirement. I worked at the AFL for six years after I officially retired, with involvement in game development and coaching the national team. Presently, I'm working as List Manager in the AFL system, in control of overseeing recruitment, the lists and the contracting process for our players … so maybe some might say I am not quite retired? Basically, I am obviously still heavily involved in something I love: football. So I reckon I'm lucky, in lots of ways.

The outcome of my story is a real positive I think. And, in telling it, I am happy to be able to tell whoever wants to read this that being with an Australian company such as Custodian did help when we needed it. Custodian has been a great journey for us.

One we're still on. We have a lovely home in Melbourne … still with a little debt sitting on it, but the program is a 'ways and means' by which we have been able to set ourselves up. We have two young boys, so beyond primary school we have education costs to consider with them. All told, we plan to continue with Custodian, as we know that's our way forward.

My life and work are busy, but we all do need to make sure to get some time away. After what I went through, and after what Nerissa went through with me, I know it's important to get away, spend some time with the family—overseas or anywhere in Australia—and do the things you love. Custodian is the road by which we can do these things and I hope to continue to do more.

Jason McCartney

Let's recap

- It's the starting that stops most people, or as Lao Tzu said 'the journey of 1000 miles begins with one step'. You will never know your potential until you take that step.

- When I started building wealth it was for me, but my motivation changed when I had reached a comfort level and the real 'why' emerged.

- When we started Toogoolawa we had a home for three homeless kids. We now have a school for more than 100 boys excluded from mainstream school.

- At Toogoolawa we believe that before we can engage the head with the students we must engage the heart.

- Jason McCartney has been successfully using the '7 steps strategy' for 20 years despite lots of change in his life. It works.

APPENDIX A

Tenancy application form

Rent Payment

☑ Direct Debit is our preferred rent payment method and is a free option for tenants.
A Direct Debit form will be provided to you at the Tenancy sign up. Please speak to your property manager about other payment options if required.

Applicants Checklist

Before I submit this application, I/we have:

☐ Attached photocopies of supporting documents (see below)

☐ Inspected the property both internally and externally

☐ Completed all details in full on the application form

☐ Provided all contact details and documentation for confirmation of income source

☐ Read and signed all the Privacy Disclosure Statement and Privacy Consent

Supporting Documentation

When submitting an application you must include at least one item from
each section per applicant

Section One	**Section Two**	**Section Three**
Drivers Licence	Current Pay Slips	Previous 4 rent
Proof of Age Card	(minimum of 2)	receipts (or ledger)
Passport	If new job – Letter of	Council Rates
Bank Statement	confirmation incl. salary	Motor vehicle
	Statement of Centrelink	registration
	Entitlements	Utilities or phone
		account

Address of property you are apply for

Preference 1
Preference 2

Tenancy Requirements

Length of tenancy [months]   Rent [$ per week]

Lease start date [   ]

Names of other applicants and their relationship to you (husband, wife,
partner, friend)

[   ]

Names & ages of children (if any) [   ]

No. of pets (including breed & age) [   ]

Do you own an investment property in Australia?   Yes / No

PRIMARY CONTACT

First Name		Last Name		Email	
Phone		Mobile		Date of birth	
Drivers Licence No.	State of issue		Passport No.		Country of issue
Number of vehicles	Car rego				

Emergency Contact

Please provide an emergency contact not living with you (eg: Next of Kin)

Name	Relationship to you	Contact phone
Address		

Current Address Details

If owner occupier include details here

Current Rent / mortgage $ per week		How long have you lived there? years months	
Current address			
Agent / Landlord	Phone		Fax
Email	Reason for leaving		
Was you bond refunded in full? Yes / No	If No, please specifiy		

Previous Rental Details

Rent $ per week		How long have you lived there? years months	
Property address			
Agent / Landlord	Phone		Fax
Was you bond refunded in full? Yes / No	If No, please specifiy		

Current Employment/Self Employed

If less than 6 months in current job please also provide previous employment details.

Company Name	Your position
Payroll or Accountant	Payroll/Accountant work phone
Company address	Net income (after tax) $ per wk / fn / mth
Length of employment	Business Type/ABN (if applicable)

Student

Are you a full time student? Yes / No	TAFE / University	Student No.
Contact name	Contact No.	
Do you receive income from your parents? Yes / No	Amount $ per week	
Name of parents	Phone	

Centrelink Benefits

Type	$ per fortnight

Additional source of income

Type	$ per wk / fn / mth

Personal Referee (cannot be related)

Referees Name	Occupation
Relationship to you	Phone

APPLICANT TWO
(for additional applicants please copy this page)

First Name		Last Name		Email	
Phone		Mobile		Date of birth	
Drivers Licence No.	State of issue		Passport No.	Country of issue	
Number of vehicles	Car rego				

Emergency Contact
Please provide an emergency contact not living with you (eg: Next of Kin)

Name	Relationship to you	Contact phone
Address		

Current Address Details
(if different to the Primary contact)

If owner occupier include details here

Current Rent/mortgage $ per week		How long have you lived there? years months	
Current address			
Agent / Landlord	Phone	Fax	
Email	Reason for leaving		
Was you bond refunded in full? Yes / No	If No, please specifiy		

Previous Rental Details
(if different to the Primary contact)

Rent $ per week		How long have you lived there? years months	
Property address			
Agent / Landlord	Phone	Fax	
Was you bond refunded in full? Yes / No	If No, please specifiy		

Current Employment/Self Employed

If less than 6 months in current job please also provide previous employment details.

Company Name	Your position
Payroll or Accountant	Payroll/Accountant work phone
Company address	Net income (after tax) $ per wk / fn / mth
Length of employment	Business Type/ABN (if applicable)

Student

Are you a full time student? Yes / No	TAFE / University	Student No.
Contact name	Contact No.	
Do you receive income from your parents? Yes / No	Amount $ per week	
Name of parents	Phone	

Centrelink Benefits

Type	$ per fortnight

Additional source of income

Type	$ per wk / fn / mth

Personal Referee (cannot be related)

Referees Name	Occupation
Relationship to you	Phone

Confirmation

I confirm that during my inspection of this property I found it to be in a satisfactory condition and suitable for occupancy.

If No, I believe the following items should be attended to prior to the commencement of my tenancy. I acknowledge and understand that these items are subject to the landlord's approval and do not form part of the Tenancy Agreement.

I also acknowledge that this rental application is subject to the Landlord's approval and I consent to the information provided in this application being verified and a reference check on VEDA being undertaken.

Primary contact

Name: .... Signature: .... Date: ....

Applicant two

Name: .... Signature: .... Date: ....

Source: Little Real Estate

APPENDIX B

Questions and answers

This is where, as promised, I answer some of the 'Yes, but...' and 'What if...?' questions that people often bring to our seminars. I don't want to put doubts in your mind where none may have existed, but you may find this appendix helpful for added confidence—or perhaps as a prompt to other questions you'll want to ask as you investigate the wealth-building concept further.

I have arranged the queries in alphabetical order by topic, so you can use this as a quick reference tool as things occur to you.

At the end of this appendix you'll also find the answers to the quiz at the start of Part I.

Economic cycles

Q: What if property doesn't go up by as much as it has done in the past—or even falls in value?

A: See Step 5.

Goods and services tax

Q: If I acquire properties and rent them out for residential use, do I need to collect GST?

A: Without getting too technical, from a GST perspective residential rent is input taxed. This essentially means that a residential landlord is not required to collect GST on residential rent.

The residential landlord will, however, *pay* GST when incurring expenses associated with the property such as repairs and maintenance, and agent's fees. The residential landlord will not be able to claim a GST input tax credit for the GST included in these expenses. The total amount of the expense, however, including the amount of GST, will be allowed as an income tax deduction.

While this may increase the landlord's operating expenses, it is anticipated that rents will gradually increase to take account of the flow-through effect of the GST.

The good news is that GST should have a positive impact on the value of property in Australia.

Inability to find a tenant

Q: What if I can't get a tenant for my property?

A: See Step 2; and 'Loss of tenant' on page 179.

Interest rates

Q: What if interest rates increase?

A: The good news is that when interest rates increase, it means that the economy is moving, and your property is going up in value, and so are rents. The bad news is, your costs are increasing too.

One solution is to lock in your loans: all of them, or a percentage of your portfolio, at any time. Establish with your bank, when you begin your wealth-building program, that you'd like to have the flexibility to lock in a rate at any time, or a percentage of your total portfolio loan, given that you may float some as variable and some as fixed. The fixed rate for five years is generally around 1 per cent more than the variable rate. (This may seem a small amount, but you should be looking at each percentage point as costing you $60 to $70 per week in cash going out of your pocket, so you need to watch it very, very closely.)

Don't be greedy. If you are comfortable with your repayments as they are now, why not lock in?

Loan problems

Q: What if the bank won't lend me the money for a further property on the equity I've got?

A: Basically, you can either wait—or change banks. Find one that will accept the equity position you want. Make sure you clearly flag your intentions to build a portfolio on this basis (see Step 4). Don't be surprised if you have to change banks two or three times in your wealth-building journey. Banks are often more aggressive about winning new business than about keeping existing clients.

Loss of employment

Q: What if I lose my job?

A: People on PAYG Income Tax Withholding are often concerned that they may lose their job, and—having built up a portfolio of two, three or four properties—may have to sell in the midst of a down cycle (or worse) while simultaneously losing the income advantages of varying the amount of their PAYG Income Tax Withholding.

Okay, put like that, it sounds pretty bad. But you can *insure* against losing your job, if it is a realistic concern in your circumstances or area of employment. You might choose to investigate this insurance. However, the simpler option is to 'self-insure', by simply slowing down your wealth-building program.

It's not a race to acquire six properties. If it takes eight, 10 or 12 years, it's not going to make a great deal of difference in the long run. For peace of mind, if you have a job that you feel is not 100 per cent secure, just be a little less aggressive in your expansion program for the time being. You may want to have a bit more equity in one property before you acquire the next. Perhaps, rather than starting at 10 per cent equity, start at 20 to 25 per cent. This is not a reason to do *nothing*!

There may be another option. As an employer, I invite my staff to let me know if they are thinking of acquiring an investment property, so that I can give them honest, forward-looking information about their job. Might your employer be amenable to such a discussion?

Loss of tenant

Q: What if my tenants leave suddenly—or damage the property?

A: It's inevitable that you're going to lose a tenant or two over a 10- to 12-year period. And if you do lose a tenant, it may take you a couple of weeks to clean the place up and find another one. This is just a factor of the rental income business. Get used to the idea—and plan accordingly.

I forecast my income based on 48 to 49 weeks' rent per year. I also keep a two-week contingency fund in the account for each property—just for incidentals (or 'accidentals').

You can have some assurance. Get a bond from all tenants of at least one month's rent, and require that they pay their rent in advance: preferably monthly, but at least fortnightly. If they're late with their rent, the agent should be on alert to advise you within one or two days, so that arrangements can be made with the tenant, or—if they are having longer term financial difficulties—so that notices can be given and the property can be inspected. If tenants wish, they can evade paying rent for up to six weeks, so you might lose up to two week's rent. This is insurable, however.

Assuming that tenants have done *everything* in the Nightmare Tenants' Handbook, they could leave you with a few thousand dollars' worth of damage that has to be repaired. *Still* not a reason to panic: this is also insurable, except for your excess, which you can limit to $250. The important thing is, don't wait for the claim: get in and clean the property up as soon as the tenant is evicted. Make sure you get quotes and send them to the insurance company—and *get on with getting your property rented again*, as soon as possible.

In my experience, it comes down to financial management and having that little bit in reserve tucked away for a rainy day. Losing a bad tenant may seem, for a while, like that rainy day, but (a) it is *not* personal—it happens to all of us; and (b) to be honest, 'good riddance'! It's *not* a good reason to wash your hands of a residential portfolio—or the wealth that comes with it!

Management hassles

Q: Isn't managing one rental property—let alone a whole portfolio—a major hassle?

A: Not necessarily—and *not* if you get someone else to do it for you!

The choice of agent to manage your property is one of the most important you'll make. Often, would-be landlords fall into the trap of going with the agent who offers them the highest rent: this is not necessarily an indicator of ability to manage a property successfully.

The questions to ask of a prospective agent are the same you'd ask of prospective employees. Who have they worked for before? What references do they have?

In essence, look for agents who (a) have experience in managing a large rent roll, (b) have limited vacancies for any given period of time, and (c) have managed on behalf of landlords for an extensive period of time.

Don't be shy about asking for half a dozen references (or more!) and make sure you ring them *all*. Include a reference from at least one landlord whose property is vacant at the time: such clients will often give you a clear insight into any agent you are looking to appoint.

The other important point to determine is exactly what the agent is going to do for you, and how much it is going to cost you. Generally, the agent's job will fall into the following categories:

- furnishing you with a fully itemised monthly statement

- conducting full internal and external inspections prior to letting—and every three months, along with photographs of the property and a written report

- providing direct payment of rent received (within three days of the new month) into the bank account of your choice, or by cheque posted directly to you

- lodging all bonds with the Bond Board, paying accounts (with your permission and on your behalf) and attending to all leases and notices pertaining to the property

- liaising with all tradespeople and inspecting all work prior to payment

- attending to final inspection on your behalf, prior to the expiry of your three-month new home maintenance warranty

- checking all potential tenants' references prior to consulting with you on their acceptability.

Most competent agents will do all of the above for you, and will include it in their management fee.

Tax law changes

Q: What if the government abolishes negative gearing?

A: In July 1985, the federal labor government disallowed the tax benefits of negative gearing. All losses that were generated had to be rolled up into the cost of the property and deducted, at the time the property was sold, from the capital gains tax. Panic!

Well, actually, no. The change to the accounting process wasn't too disastrous for investors at the time, because it *wasn't retrospective*: anyone who owned negatively geared properties prior to 1985 could continue claiming the deductions. More importantly, however, the change in policy caused a *major* stall in investment in the new residential property market. Suddenly, there was a looming (drastic) shortage in the supply of residential housing for a growing rental population, and an economy-dragging downturn in building activity.

The treasurer was forced to *reintroduce* negative gearing in September 1987. Any residential property investor who purchased properties during the two-year abolition period was allowed to offset their two-year losses against their assessable income for 1987–88 (nice u-turn).

Negative gearing hit the political agenda again, with the revelation that people had been using the provisions to purchase *shares*: the government was considering re-abolishing negative gearing to close the loophole.

But in 1997, the then Prime Minister, John Howard, made a statement that: 'Negative gearing would not be abolished on residential property'.

Of course, all we can do is work on the knowledge available to us now, and that is:

- you *can* legitimately negatively gear property
- the government is unlikely to abolish negative gearing on residential property in the future because of the proven knock-on effects on housing supply and economic activity

- if the government *did* abolish it again, it probably wouldn't be done retrospectively, so any purchase that you made today should be within the safety net of today's taxation laws.

With the introduction of the GST and other taxation reform measures, the government has only reviewed negative gearing by disallowing investors to claim travel costs among some other minor clawbacks. The Commissioner of Taxation, however, has released several rulings in an attempt to restrict split loans, redraw facilities and capitalisation of interest expenses. Investors may be prevented from borrowing 150 to 200 per cent of the property's value over a period of time and negatively gearing on that amount. This would not, in fact, affect our wealth-building structure at all.

Noise, noise, noise. At every election, and certainly during a property boom, the issue of affordability and negative gearing comes up. Liberals, who are in government as I write, had a hard look at negative gearing and decided to make no changes. However, Labor has decided to abolish negative gearing on second-hand properties. This actually does not affect the structure in *7 Steps to Wealth*, but you'll hear a lot of noise.

Labor's argument is that the (nearly) two million Australians who have an investment property and are using negative gearing for second-hand properties are not adding to the economy or providing new homes for our population. Their logic is that if negative gearing is only restricted to new purchases, it will help supply and affordability. That's a theory and we won't know the answer to that until Labor rules that law in for 10 to 20 years. What is important to us is that Labor said that they *will* grandfather existing negatively geared property, and their modelling shows that over a 10-year period, a lot of investors will have sold their property anyway. So the benefits of the taxation system won't kick in for 10 years.

Irrespective, the strategy I put forward in *7 Steps to Wealth* is building a land bank and using new property so that you can get the tax benefits (which I've been saying for 20 years). So nothing I've heard affects the strategy of *7 Steps to Wealth*.

Valuations

Q: What if the bank refuses to disclose its valuation?

A: This is a *must-have* piece of information. The simple answer is if one bank won't disclose the valuation to you — find another one that will.

Any other questions?

If you have *any* further 'What about…?' or 'What if…?' (or even 'Where exactly did you get that statistic on…?') questions — *great*!

I suggest you go to our 7 Steps website or call 1800 174 999. My colleagues are all fellow wealth-builders with their own land banks who can help you answer any questions you may have.

Sceptics make the best wealth-builders so we're comfortable with questions (and answers).

Quiz answers

As promised, here are the answers to the quiz from the start of Part I. Look at your answers again and review them. With all the knowledge you've gained by the reading the book, you may well want to change some of your answers.

Then compare your answers with the ones below. How did you go?

1. In making a wealth-building investment decision, what would be more important?

   ☐ how you feel about it

   ✓ how it stacks up logically

2. What has shown the higher investment return over the past 10 years?

   ☐ shares

   ✓ residential property

3. In buying a residential investment property for wealth-building, what would be most important?

   ☐ rental returns

   ☐ taxation benefits

   ✓ capital growth

4. If you invested in residential property, would you use the same criteria and decision-making process as you used to acquire your own home?

   ☐ yes

   ✓ no

5. Is it prudent for you to acquire property close to where you live?

   ☐ yes

   ✓ no

6. What would be more important when acquiring an investment property for *wealth building*?

   ✓ managing your cash flow

   ☐ buying the right property

7. What type of property would show the highest capital growth?

   ☐ unit/townhouse

   ☐ house

   ✓ land

8. If you had a $300 000 deposit to invest in property, would you be better off buying:

   ☐ one property for $1 000 000?

   ☐ one property for $2 000 000?

   ✓ two properties for $500 000 each?

9. The median house price in Brisbane rose from $30 500 in 1977 to $550 000 in 2018.

   ✓ true

   ☐ false

10. If you bought a house in 1967 in Melbourne, Sydney or Brisbane, by how much would its value have increased in 2017?

   ☐ doubled in value

   ☐ five times (500%)

   ☐ 10 times (1000%)

   ☐ 20 times (2000%)

   ✓ 50 times (5000%)

11. Which institution(s) effectively control the affordability of housing in Australia?

   ☐ the Real Estate Institute

   ✓ banks

   ☐ property developers

   ☐ valuers

12. Is the number of renters of property in Australia increasing or decreasing?

    ✓ increasing

    ☐ decreasing

13. The Pay As You Go (PAYG) income tax (including Medicare Levy) on a salary of $60 000 is approximately $12 250.

    ✓ true

    ☐ false

14. Can I use my PAYG tax to build wealth?

    ✓ yes

    ☐ no

15. In choosing a location that is going to give capital growth, which factor is most important?

    ☐ proximity to transport

    ☐ proximity to schools

    ☐ percentage of investor-owners

    ✓ established capital benchmark

16. You are seeking a bank loan for an investment property. Rank the following criteria in order of priority.

    4 interest rate of loan

    2 interest-only loan

    1 full disclosure of bank valuation of investment property

    3 non-collateralisation of other property

17. What is the 'established capital benchmark' of an area?

    ☐ the median price of property in the area

    ✓ the highest price of property in the area

    ☐ the lowest price of property in the area

18. What was the average land size of urban houses in Australia's capital cities in 1970?

    ☐ 450 m^2

    ☐ 600 m^2

    ☐ 750 m^2

    ✓ 1000 m^2

19. What was the average land size of urban houses in Australia's capital cities in 2017?

    ✓ 450 m^2

    ☐ 600 m^2

    ☐ 750 m^2

    ☐ 1000 m^2

20. What was the percentage growth in the median price of a typical high-rise unit between 1999 and 2017?

    ✓ 4%

    ☐ 6%

    ☐ 8%

    ☐ 10%

21. What is the fastest growing employment sector in Australia?

✓ healthcare

☐ education

☐ manufacturing

☐ retail

☐ construction

And finally

Pat yourself on the back. Seriously. Allow yourself to feel good about the knowledge and awareness you've developed. If you got some 'wrong' answers—great! That's often the best way to learn.

Especially if the whole property investment 'thing' was new to you, you may have had to take on board a load of unfamiliar terms, information and ideas. So you *know you can*. In fact, I hope you'll be reasonably confident that *you can build wealth*. You can do more—and be more—than perhaps you thought when you started reading this book.

If you've stayed with me right to the end, thanks. It gives me genuine satisfaction to have shared some of my experience and perspective with you—and to wonder what you might *do* with that information, and those ideas, and your own potential. (Feel free to drop me a line and let me know how you're going. I'd love to know—and I will reply.) I hope you will become a fellow wealth-builder and Custodian. But wherever you go from here:

May you be all you can be.

7 STEPS TO WEALTH

Now you've read the book—you

should have lots of questions.

That's good.

Meet with us to investigate

further—it's complimentary.

Start your 7 Steps journey today.

1800 174 999

sevenstepstowealth.com

A PLACE IN THE HEART
Toogoolawa
SCHOOLS

OUR COMMITMENT WITH TOOGOOLAWA SCHOOLS

More information:

toogoolawa.com.au

facebook.com/toogoolawa

If you wish to donate please

contact toogoolawa@jlf.com.au